STUDYING FILMS

student editions

STUDYING SURREALIST AND FANTASY CINEMA

Neil Coombs

181773   791·436116 COO

Neil Coombs

is a video and multimedia artist who has exhibited individual and collaborative work internationally. He is an experienced lecturer in Film and Media Studies across a range of Further and Higher education courses.

Dedication

For Ruth Coombs, Beryl Coombs and all the little Coombs's.

Acknowledgements

Thanks to John at Auteur for his support and advice, and my students past and present.

First published in 2007; revised 'student edition' first published in 2008 by Auteur, The Old Surgery, 9 Pulford Road, Leighton Buzzard LU7 1AB
www.auteur.co.uk
Copyright © Auteur 2008

Series design: Nikki Hamlett
Cover image: *Being John Malkovich* © Gramercy Pictures/Aquarius Collection
The publisher believes the following copyright information to be correct, but will be delighted to correct any errors brought to our attention in future editions.
Pages 7 (*Un chien andalou*), 21 (*L'Âge d'Or*), 29 (*Metropolis*), 63 (Bunuel), 64 and 72 (*Orphee*), 79 (*Alice*), 50 (*The City of Lost Children*) © BFI Stills; page 31 (*Eyes Without a Face*) © Gaumount; page 34 (*Ilya Muromets*) © RUSICO; page 43 (*The Phantom of Liberty*) © Studio Canal; page 94 (*Lost Highway*) © Aquarius Collection; pages 132-134 (*A History of Violence*) © First Independent; page 143 (*Being John Malkovich*) © Gramercy Pictures/Universal DVD.
Set by AMP Ltd, Dunstable, Bedfordshire
Printed and bound in Poland; produced by Polskabook

British Library Cataloguing-in-Publication Data
A catalogue record for this book is available from the British Library

ISBN 978-1-903663-96-7

Contents

Introduction

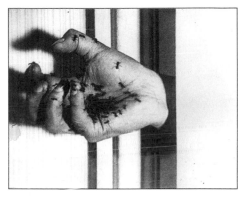

This book is intended to offer an overview of Surrealist
and fantasy film from a non-Hollywood or 'world cinema'
perspective. Surrealism was a twentieth century avant-garde
art movement that tapped into a number of elements of
modern life and had a major influence on the development
of film language and fantasy cinema. In attempting to define
Surrealist and fantasy cinema, areas of debate will emerge. As
in all good Film Studies work, there are no definitive answers
– but in debating the issues, and exploring the films and their
content, much can be learnt. You will be able to apply these
investigations to a broad range of films, using a number of
theoretical tools. *Auteur*, genre and spectatorship studies all
relate closely to this topic.

This book outlines the roots of the Surrealist movement, and
its relationship with popular culture and cinema in particular.
It considers the development of Surrealist cinema through
case studies of specific directors and their films. The book
also attempts to define the scope of fantasy cinema and
consider the difference between fantasy and Surrealist film
genres, using detailed studies of specific films. Issues relating

to narrative conventions, spectatorship, national and historical context are considered.

What is Surrealist and Fantasy Cinema?

Unlike other film movements or styles, Surrealist and fantasy cinema is not limited by national or historic boundaries. This can make it a difficult topic but it could be considered an opportunity for you to relate 'difficult' world cinema to more mainstream topics covered elsewhere. The defining feature of Surrealist and fantasy cinema is that it will attempt to challenge our perceptions of reality by rejecting conventional ways of telling stories and structuring narratives. These films will develop new technical and representational conventions to explore psychological and social issues.

There is a subtle difference between Surrealist and fantasy as cinematic categories that can be best summed up by examining the roots of Surrealism as an ideology. Surrealist cinema is designed to provoke a response; to challenge and attack the conventions of society. Fantasy film may have surreal *elements* but will not have the same intention to change or undermine society. Surrealism is essentially intending to be provocative and revolutionary; fantasy can just as easily be conventional and reactionary.

Many mainstream films are 'fantasy' films but are also very conventional in their use of narrative and the issues that they explore. It is therefore important to be careful in selecting films for study as examples of fantasy texts. A film such as *The Matrix* (1999) is a good example of a mainstream Hollywood fantasy production as it uses narrative and technical innovations to explore issues of reality and perception; whereas a film such as *Star Wars* (1977) is much more traditional in its narrative and psychological concerns. For the Surrealist revolutionary, where both of these films fail is in their need to fit the demands of the Hollywood marketing system; therefore, if *The Matrix* has been studied as an example of film as a product in contemporary Hollywood, it can be considered in relation to a film such as *The City of Lost Children* (1995) that has different institutional roots.

How to Approach the Subject

As the topic of Surrealist and fantasy cinema is not tied to one particular historical period or one national cinema, it may seem difficult to identify a way to approach the subject as a distinct case study. Surrealist film can profitably be used towards the end of a Film Studies course in order to apply some of the critical tools developed in other areas:

1. The conventions of narrative cinema and Hollywood film language can be considered in the ways that they are confronted and adapted to surreal ends.

2. A study of the horror, science fiction or fantasy genres could be developed to consider surreal cinema.

3. Audience study, censorship and 'shocking cinema' are general topics that could feed into a study of some of the more controversial elements of Surrealist film.

4. *Auteur* theory could be used to investigate one of the more popular directors mentioned (David Lynch or David Cronenberg, for example); this study could be expanded to examine the influence of Buñuel and the Surrealists.

When first approaching this topic, it is worth initially introducing general definitions of Surrealism and fantasy film, exploring the historical context by examining extracts from a range of films and television sources. (These could be films that have been covered previously, revisited to look at their surreal or fantasy elements. Dream sequences from mainstream films are good examples to use, as are television adverts that attempt to work on a subconscious level or surreal comedy shows.)

After this initial introduction and contextualisation, you can choose one Surrealist film from the case studies in this book and analyse its use of narrative conventions, character types, themes and film language. You could then progress to look at the similarities and differences between Surrealism and fantasy film. In a nutshell, Surrealist films are films that develop the themes of the subconscious, the irrational and chance, using these themes to question moral, social or psychological truths. They have surreal content used to a specific, radical, end. Fantasy films tend to deal with the boundary between reality and the supernatural – they occupy the space between waking and dreaming where we are not certain of the nature of reality.

David Cronenberg wants to 'show the unshowable' (Rodley, 1992. p. xviii); Buñuel wants to suggest the unknowable. Fantasy is often escapist whereas Surrealism tends to be grounded in reality whilst making us question that reality. Fantasy will usually have a clearly structured narrative; Surrealism will have intentionally disjointed or unresolved narratives. Fantasy will use clearly defined archetypal characters with a character arc (or an oedipal trajectory); Surrealism will have characters as social stereotypes that are 'acted upon' by situations. In Surrealism the characters are not able to drive the narrative; they are acted upon by the story.

One interesting approach is to look at how the topic infiltrates other topics and connects to other areas of Film Studies. Below is a brief suggested outline as to how this topic might relate to other areas you have studied.

Exploring Film Form:

Film Language (micro): You will have been introduced to the conventions of Hollywood film language. This could be developed into a consideration of how these conventions have been used in mainstream fantasy film to make possible explorations of psychological states (suggested example: detailed textual analysis of a fantasy sequence from *Eternal Sunshine of the Spotless Mind*, 2004).

Film Language (macro): You will have been introduced to the conventions of genre and narrative. If you were to investigate the horror genre, you could explore the psychological motivation of characters and the idea of 'the subconscious' as a generic element in mainstream Hollywood.

Practical Work: If you are creating a short storyboard, script or film as part of your course, you could attempt to create a dream sequence using Surrealist techniques.

Producers and Audiences:

The Film Industry: You could investigate fantasy film as a product in contemporary Hollywood, considering a fantasy franchise such as *The Matrix* in comparison to more alternative or experimental Hollywood films such as *Southland Tales* (2006). You may want to consider industrial issues such as the way that non-linear narratives feed into the development of ancillary markets, computer games and alternative methods of distribution. Another way to consider surrealism and the subconscious is to examine how the advertising and marketing of films plays upon our subconscious desires

The Film Audience: The notion of film as a cultural experience allows us to consider our own fantasies, suspension of disbelief and the expectations we have of a cinematic experience. There are also opportunities to consider the ways in which Hollywood stars and the cult of celebrity affect our own sense of identity.

British Cinema: Studying British cinema allows us to look at realism which can be later considered in relation to Surrealism. If we focus on 1960s British cinema we can see how films such as *Performance* (1970), *If...* (1968) and *A Hard Day's Night* (1964) effectively combine realist techniques with fantasy elements to surreal effect. Polanski's *Repulsion* (1965) is another interesting film from this period to consider in terms of its subtly surreal atmosphere.

British Case Study: *The Wicker Man* (1973) is a good film to pull together some of the issues discussed above: it uses relatively conventional film language and is from the horror genre; it deals with social taboos and the subconscious; and it has a conventional narrative yet manages to convey a surreal mood.

Research or Creative Projects

As part of your Film Studies course, you will be expected to carry out research projects and practical work. Surrealist and fantasy cinema can be a useful topic to form the basis of either of these.

For example: Consideration of either Luis Buñuel, David Lynch or David Cronenberg as an auteur with an opportunity to develop some of the themes and ideas from their work into a practical project of your own (you could attempt to create a 'Buñuelian' or 'Lynchian' film based on your own personal experience and understanding of their authorial technique).

Issues and Debates

Surrealism allows you to consider a range of issues and debates that you will have investigated over the course of your studies.

International Film Style: Surrealist and fantasy film can be considered as an example of a film movement or style. You could investigate the history and roots of Surrealism (relating this to work that you have covered previously). You may want to carry out close textual analysis of key Surrealist or fantasy texts. This could develop into an exploration of the legacy and influence of Surrealism on world and Hollywood cinema.

Contemporary World Cinema: Films from recent years could be used to develop some of the issues that have arisen through the study of Surrealist and fantasy cinema: *Talk to Her* (2002) could be examined to consider how issues that were important to the Surrealists (such as sexual taboos and the Catholic church) can be developed through the techniques of melodrama. *Anatomy of Hell* (2004) has poetic, elements as well as dealing explicitly with the issue of sexual desire and voyeurism (again important to the Surrealists). A DOGME film such as *The Idiots* (1998) could be considered as an example of a response to a contemporary manifesto, *You, The Living* (2007) could be explored in relation to narrative - a recent film that relates to Buñuel's *Phantom of Liberty* in its surreal, episodic structure.

Spectatorship: As outlined in this book, spectatorship study is important to any study of surreal cinema. The study of shocking cinema can be a useful way to develop issues previously addressed (suggested example: David Cronenberg's *Crash*, 1996). Experimental film-making can also be a useful case study to develop Surrealist themes and issues while investigating the broader context of non-mainstream cinema. The emotional responses created by surrealist cinema – the shock effect of *Un Chien Andalou* or the unsettling nature of *Lost Highway* are interesting examples.

Gendered Film Studies: A review of surreal and fantasy films from the perspective of the 'male gaze' and objectification may lead to questions about how revolutionary Surrealist films really are.

1. What is Surrealism?

Surrealism and 'the surreal' are terms that are quite regularly used in film and television reviews. A glance through any weekly listing magazine will normally include references to comedies, dramas and even documentaries that are described as 'surreal'. Of all the twentieth century cultural movements, surrealism has become the most accessible or relevant to contemporary living: 'surreal' is used by many in everyday conversation. We all have our own understanding of the term and use it in a range of ways. As a starting point in studying surreal and fantasy cinema, it may be worth considering what surrealism means to us as individuals by carrying out 'surreal activities' (see below). In order to investigate Surrealist and fantasy cinema we need to understand the origins of the surrealist movement and its aims and influences.

Dada and the Roots of Surrealism

It is important firstly to define surrealism and position it in a historical context. Surrealism was a cultural movement that had its roots in a previous art movement called 'Dada'. Dada is relevant to surrealist cinema as the aims and methods of the surrealists developed from the work of Dada artists and many of the founders of the surrealist movement were associated with the Dada group.

The Dada was a radical group of artists who had no real common stylistic identity – the art they produced took a number of different forms from poems to performances. The Dada artists shared an opposition to the First World War (1914–18) and the dominant culture of the time. They wanted to create art that had radical political ideas as the main content, rather than craft skills and middle class values.

Dada developed in a number of places and a range of personalities were associated with the movement but it was first given its name in 1916, in the city of Zurich, Switzerland. It was the middle of the First World War and Switzerland was a neutral country at the heart of Europe. The Dada artists established themselves in a relatively safe environment while all around the mechanised slaughter of the first modern war was changing the world's perception of national and social relations.

The majority of the art and culture of the time promoted various forms of nationalism, romanticism and religion; seeming to ignore the reality of life for the soldiers and civilians living and dying in the heart of the 'civilised world'. The Dada artists held performances of music and poetry at a club in Zurich called the Cabaret Voltaire. Although Dada paintings and sculptures were created, the work of the Dada artists mainly existed as gestures and provocative public performances.

Over the years, the spirit of Dada has been revisited and has informed a range of nihilistic cultural movements, the most obvious being punk in the late 1970s. Much of the graphic style and attitude of punk music and culture grew from the ideas of the Dada artists. When Jamie Reid put a safety pin through Queen Elizabeth II's face on the cover art for the Sex Pistols' 'God Save the Queen', it was a similar to Marcel Duchamp's iconoclastic image of the Mona Lisa with a moustache and beard pencilled on.

Manifestos

A manifesto is a statement of the ideals and intent of a political or cultural movement. We are used to political parties issuing manifestos that outline policies; nowadays these tend to be anything but radical and read more like extended advertisement features. In the late nineteenth and early twentieth centuries there were many manifestos authored by small groups of people intending to develop a following; outlining a solution to the perceived ills of the world and inspiring others to join their organisation in order to change the world. Karl Marx and Frederich Engels' *Communist Manifesto* is probably the most famous and influential in twentieth century history.

The writings of the Dada artists were less scientific and more open to interpretation than the radical political manifestos of the nineteenth and twentieth centuries but shared the same desire: to change the world through action. The Dada artists could see the problems but refused to offer clear solutions:

'I am writing a manifesto and there's nothing I want, and yet I'm saying certain things, and in principle I am against manifestos as I am against principles.' (Tzara, 1918, p. 3)

There were a number of Dada manifestos signed by artists such as Hugo Ball, Hans Arp, Hans Richter and Tristan Tzara. The main intention of these statements was to agitate against the First World War and society's complacency in the face of the horrors of modern warfare.

To make the idea of manifestos relevant to contemporary Film Studies, it may be worth considering the DOGME manifesto as an example of a recent radical cultural manifesto:

'DOGME 95 is a rescue action! In 1960 enough was enough! The movie was dead and called for resurrection. The goal was correct but the means were not! The New Wave proved to be a ripple that washed ashore and turned to muck. Slogans of individualism and freedom created works for a while, but no changes. The wave was up for grabs, like the directors

themselves. The wave was never stronger than the men behind it. The anti-bourgeois cinema itself became bourgeois, because the foundations upon which its theories were based was the bourgeois perception of art. The auteur *concept was bourgeois romanticism from the very start and thereby ... false! To DOGME 95 cinema is not individual!'* (von Trier & Vinterberg, DOGME Manifesto, 1995)

The spirit of Dada moved to Paris and Berlin after the war. Andre Bréton (who was to become the chief architect of Surrealism) joined the group in Paris, while in Germany artists such as Max Ernst, Kurt Schwitters and John Heartfield got involved. They developed techniques of collage (Schwitters' 'Merz') and photomontage (Heartfield's anti-Nazi works). Marcel Duchamp (the architect of the 'Readymade' in art) was also associated with the movement and moved to New York where his work inspired Pop Art and Abstract Expressionism.

Two film-makers joined the Dada group in Zurich: Hans Richter and Viking Eggeling. They made films using paper cut-outs and basic animation techniques; they wanted to escape from the naturalistic style of early films and create a new abstract pictorial language. Eggeling died at the age of 45 in 1920, but Richter continued to make films and in 1947 he directed *Dreams That Money Can Buy*, a film about a man who sells dreams (his customers being well-known Surrealist artists). Man Ray is famous as a photographer but also made films including the Dada-influenced *Le Retour à la raison* (1923). In Paris, René Clair made the Dada film *Entr'acte* (1924), a combination of abstract forms and slapstick sequences. The absence of a conventional Hollywood narrative points the way towards later Surrealist films.

Surrealism (introducing the revolutionary power of the unconscious)

André Breton is seen as the founder of Surrealism and published his Surrealist manifesto in Paris in 1924. This manifesto was aimed at poets and did not address the visual arts or film (which was still a relatively new medium).

The Surrealists took the spirit of Dada (using unconscious activity and nonsense for creative and revolutionary ends) and developed a more scientific approach to using 'the unconscious' in the creation of art. They had a more positive approach than the Dada artists: they saw art as a means with which to change society for the better. Breton was himself influenced by Sigmund Freud who had published *The Interpretation of Dreams* in 1900. (Breton met Freud in 1921 but Freud was not keen on having his theories used for artistic ends.)

The Surrealists were concerned with liberating the unconscious – they questioned social, moral and religious conventions through questioningconventional language structures, including visual and film language as well as dress codes and behavioural codes.

The Surrealists were initially a literary movement, interested in poetry and language. Painting was not a major area of interest. The Surrealists were more interested in developing language (in its broadest sense, including film language) through hypnosis, dreams and games as keys to revealing 'the true function of thought' (Breton, 1924, cited in Waldberg, 1971 p. 75). We can see that the Surrealist movement had developed and established itself before Salvador Dali (arguably the most famous Surrealist) joined the group in 1929.

The Surrealists broke the rules of accepted behaviour: the

social, religious and artistic taboos of their time. They felt that it was important to investigate pure thought – that through Surrealist techniques they could solve 'the principal problems of life' (Breton, 1924, cited in Waldberg, ibid.). They believed that producing art from the unconscious mind would say more about reality than conscious attempts to create art. This seems to indicate that they saw the artist as a searcher for some kind of universal truth.

Over a period of time, two main types of Surrealist art began to develop:

1. Automatism or 'stream of consciousness' poetry and drawing.

This is where ideas are allowed to develop without the control of reason or aesthetics. The Surrealists would write accounts of their dreams, take part in séances and play games such as 'the exquisite corpse' to explore the workings of the unconscious. Outside of Surrealism, the writing of James Joyce and the paintings of Jackson Pollock are examples of 'stream of consciousness' work.

2. Hyper-real representations of dream images.

These are probably the most well-known of Surrealist art works and include the paintings of Salvador Dali, René Magritte and Max Ernst. In the attempt to represent the 'true function of thought' painting as a representational technique is limited in that it lacks the time-based narrative of written stories. Conversely, written work lacks the 'plastic' imagery that dreams produce. These limitations seem to lead inevitably to the apparatus of cinema as the perfect medium for the creation of surreal art.

2. Surrealist and Fantasy Cinema

'Surrealism: A movement that dates back to the 1920s and which impacted on films of that time but which still has a small influence today – particularly in horror films. This movement, much influenced by Freud, strove to embody in art and poetry the irrational forces of dreams and the unconscious. Surrealist films are concerned with depicting the workings of the unconscious (perceived as irrational, excessive, grotesque, libidinal) and with the liberating force of unconscious desires and fantasy that are normally repressed.' (Hayward, 1996, p. 370)

Surrealists were quick to see the possibility of cinema as a means of unlocking the unconscious. The power of cinema to fully involve the viewer in a dream-like state was evident from its birth as the 'dream factory'. Surrealist cinema is able to combine both types of Surrealist art in that it uses the techniques of realist cinema to present dream-like narratives.

These narratives confront the conventions of Hollywood storytelling. They also used films to challenge the ideology of society: they included erotic and anti-religious elements that challenged socially accepted behaviour.

In Surrealist films, people acted as they would in dreams; there was little concern for conventional notions of narrative. Among other things, they were comments on the stiff and constrained dramas and self-censorship of mainstream Hollywood cinema.

The key Surrealist film-maker is the Spaniard, Luis Buñuel, who created *L'Âge d'Or* (1930) with Salvador Dali and the early Surrealist short film *Un chien andalou* (1929). These films follow the logic of dreams and their aim was to release the power of the unconscious. Their use of editing to create associations was advanced and many of the techniques developed over 70 years ago are still being appropriated by the advertising industry today. (The recent television advertising campaigns of Guinness, Tango and 3 Mobile use surreal logic to sell their products.)

In his autobiography *My Last Breath* (1983), Luis Buñuel describes how *Un chien andalou* came about after a discussion with Salvador Dali over two dreams which they took as a starting point for the film.

'When I arrived to spend a few days at Dali's house in Figueras, I told him about a dream I'd had in which a long, tapering cloud sliced the moon in half, like a razor blade slicing through an eye. Dali immediately told me that he'd seen a hand crawling with ants in a dream he'd had the previous night.' (Buñuel, 1983, p. 103)

The work of Buñuel is infused with black humour. In his films everyday events are combined with grotesque images and subversive behaviour. Quite often there is a strong element of social satire and left-wing political views. The Surrealists were opposed to capitalism and to the right-wing government in France and by 1927 they had aligned themselves with the French Communist party. By the mid-1930s, Surrealist ideas had begun to develop in Eastern Europe, particularly in Prague where a Czech Surrealist group was formed and developed over a number of years free from the constraints of commercialism, with close links to the Czechoslovakian State Communist party.

Another key film-maker from the subsequent generation of Surrealists is the Czech animator, Jan Švankmajer, whose films owe a debt to the Surrealist movement. Calling himself a 'militant Surrealist' (Donald, 1989 p. 254), Švankmajer uses Surrealism to similar political ends, attacking not only capitalism, but also subtly questioning state communism. He uses puppets, animation and live-action to create a grotesquely surreal world. His work refers to the fantasy world of fairy tales, folk art, fairground puppetry and freak shows and will be explored at length later.

Surrealism and Popular Culture

The Surrealists have always maintained a strong respect for the power of popular culture, initially in terms of the 'carnivalesque'. Fairgrounds, carnivals and popular entertainments were raised to the level of art by the Surrealist group. It is also strongly evident in Švankmajer's work and the activities of the Dada artists at the Cabaret Voltaire. The carnival and the fairground are popular forms of entertainment and places where mystery, danger and fantasy lurk in the shadows – ideal material for the Surrealists' interests in the unconscious.

Surrealists were interested in popular culture (carnivals, boxing, popular music, pornography and cinema) despite the fact that:

Popular culture was (and possibly still is) seen as valueless by the cultural elite. It is worth considering what is seen as high culture and popular culture in the present day – how much has this changed in recent years?

Many radicals see popular culture as capitalist ideology created to dupe 'the masses'. This is another interesting issue of debate; for example, one could regard punk or rap music as packaged rebellion sold as a commodity.

The new medium of the motion picture appealed to the Surrealists; they were cinematic spectators and fans before they were film-makers. The early Surrealists would wander from one Parisian cinema to another, catching random snatches of narratives and re-combining them in their minds to create fractured, disjointed stories. This is similar to modern day multi-channel television channel hopping. It can also be seen in the work of a director such as Quentin Tarantino, who famously worked in a video-rental store absorbing a broad range of popular and arthouse films. Using all of these references and ideas he was able to create a style that has become ever more fantastic with the *Kill Bill* movies (2003–4).

Where does Surrealism Live Now?

Although many mainstream films have fantasy and dream sequences, there are a few Hollywood film-makers such as David Lynch and Spike Jonze who create films that develop the Surrealist's notions of the power of dreams and automatism. European cinema continues to produce Surrealist and fantasy directors such as Béla Tarr, Jean-Pierre Jeunet, Marc Caro and Roy Andersson.

The advertising industry is very keen to appeal to our subconscious in the selling of products. It is worth examining the above mentioned advertising campaigns of Guinness or Tango to see how the language of Surrealism can be used in the name of industrial commercialism. When tobacco advertising was restricted from associating its product with health or glamour, it swiftly turned to using Surrealist imagery; particularly in the Benson & Hedges and Silk Cut campaigns of the 1980s.

Surreal comedy has been successful on television: *Monty Python's Flying Circus* is probably the most well known example of Surrealist comedy (building on 'The Goons' radio show of the 1950s and even earlier music hall acts). The mantle of surreal comedy has been taken up by among others, Harry Hill, *The League of Gentlemen* and Chris Morris' *Jam*. The first series of *The League of Gentlemen* featured a cow in a bedroom, very reminiscent of a similar scene in *L'Âge d'Or*.

In concluding this brief outline of the roots and influences of Surrealism, it is worth summarising the following:

- Surrealism was a historical movement in art less concerned with painting than with the goal of unleashing the unconscious and questioning moral and social conventions.

- Over the past 75 years, there have been a number of film-makers who claim to be working as Surrealists, developing the language and scope of Surrealism.

- Surrealism has strong links with popular culture and can be seen in forms such as comedy (which also has strong links with the unconscious).

- Surrealism becomes more and more relevant as technology forces us to work on the unconscious level.

- Surrealism isn't really an 'ism' – it is more a way of (re)interpreting life and therefore can appear in many cultures and many historical periods.

What is Fantasy Film?

Fantasy film is a fairly broad category and could include the majority of mainstream film genres. The Hollywood studio system at its height was known as the 'dream factory' and since its inception cinema has been concerned with recreating fantasy and the spectacular. Similarly, there is a tradition of fantasy in Asian cinema: much of India's Bollywood output could be considered fantasy in the tradition of Hollywood's 'Golden Age'. Martial arts films from Japan, Korea and Hong Kong are often based on myths, legends and folk tales with fantasy sequences and characters. Either of these areas deserve a book of their own, and they may be considered in relation to this topic, particularly considering their growing popularity and international influence (for example *Crouching Tiger, Hidden Dragon*, 2000, *Hero*, 2002, *Bride & Prejudice*, 2004). In order to narrow the scope of this study, however, we are mainly considering fantasy cinema produced outside of mainstream Hollywood film-making in Europe and Canada.

Fantasy films are often seen in opposition to realism. This may be a good starting point at which to consider fantasy cinema but it is rather simplistic as fantasy tends to deal very directly with our internal reality – our dreams and subconscious fantasies that are just as 'real' as our physical reality. This is not the place for a debate about the nature of reality, but we should always be aware that realist cinema is equally an artificial construct.

Fantasy films are seen as unreal and are therefore able to create a paradigm into which we are drawn; a world with its own internal logic where we are able to accept fantastic situations and creatures as being plausible. The key concept here that applies to all cinematic spectatorship is the 'suspension of disbelief'. This refers to the way that, when watching a film, we are aware that we are watching a constructed story but we respond to it as if it were real. As long as the diegetic world of the film makes sense, we are willing to accept that men can fly, be reborn, walk through walls or change into insects.

In fantasy films, we enter the film's world and follow its logic. Film franchises as diverse as *Lord of the Rings* (2001–3), *The Matrix* or *Star Wars* depict worlds that are fantastical, with concepts and physical laws far removed from our reality. Yet because the world of the film makes sense as an enclosed system and has a clear (if complex) structure, we are willing to happily accept all manner of fantastic situations.

Tzvetan Todorov (in Gelder, 2000, p. 18) defined the fantastic as *'that hesitation experienced by a person who knows only the laws of nature, confronting an apparently supernatural event'*. It is interesting to consider a precise definition of such a broad term but we also need to consider that, as Todorov said, *'a genre is defined in relation to the genres adjacent to it'* (in Gelder, 2000, p. 16).

Fantasy Genres

As 'fantasy' is such an all-encompassing term in relation to film, it is worth considering which genres are most closely associated with the term. The obvious genres are those which are more avowedly anti-realist (although one could argue that romantic comedies and other light-hearted film genres fit the description just as well). In this book, we will concentrate on the following genres:

- Science fiction.

- Horror.

- Fantasy (films based on myths, legends or fantasy literature).

It is difficult to distinguish these three genres as being entirely separate, as there are many examples of mixed genre films: science fiction films will often have horror and fantasy elements, and themes and styles will often cross-over between different movies. I will briefly outline the history of each genre as a distinct category. These histories are necessarily selective and point the way to some examples from Hollywood and world cinema that might offer links to other parts of the Film Studies syllabus.

Science Fiction

The first science fiction films were produced in the silent era by Georges Méliès, whose most well known films are his *Voyages Fantastique* (1902), about journeys to the moon and the centre of the earth. These films were based on the literature of Jules Verne who wrote novels praising the developments of scientific investigation and projecting them into the future with a relatively utopian zeal. Another strand of science fiction is exemplified by H. G. Wells whose dystopian visions saw science as bringing about various forms of destruction. There were relatively few science fiction films

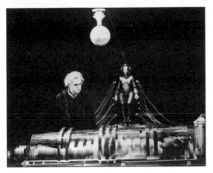

made prior to the 1950s, perhaps the most enduring being Fritz Lang's *Metropolis* (1927) which envisions a future society founded on slavery.

In the 1950s, with the Cold War at its height, the science fiction genre began to develop in Hollywood with a series of B-movies (wonderfully parodied in Tim Burton's *Mars Attacks!*, 1996). These films were relatively low budget and dealt with alien threats in the form of mysterious diseases, invaders from outer space or strange plants. The American films of this period can be read as reflecting the fear of Communism fostered by McCarthyism but also as commenting on the political paranoia that had caused the 'witch-hunt'. In Japan, the Toho Studios produced a series of 'creature features' with monsters such as *Godzilla* making regular cinematic outings throughout the 1950s and 1960s. These films make fairly unambiguous reference to the atomic attack on Japan that brought World War Two to a close.

In 1968 Stanley Kubrick made *2001: A Space Odyssey* in which technology is again seen as the potential enemy of mankind. Kubrick's vision was realised by ground-breaking special effects and a budget not previously associated with the genre. The film had its Cold War response in Andrei Tarkovsky's *Solyaris* (1972) who also made the dystopian science fiction film *Stalker* (1979).

The 1970s and 80s saw the development of science fiction as a big-budget mainstream film genre. The success of *Star*

Wars led other directors to see the mass market potential of the science fiction genre, for example, Steven Spielberg's *E.T. the Extra-Terrestrial* (1982). In this period science fiction series from TV and comic books were revived and given the blockbuster treatment, *Star Trek: The Motion Picture* (1979), *Superman* (1978) and *Flash Gordon* (1980) being good examples.

The year 1979 saw the release of *Alien* in which science fiction and horror merged with an underpinning fear of sexuality and genetic manipulation replacing the traditional fears of alien forces and mechanised technology. This was followed shortly by *The Terminator* (1984), which allowed Arnold Schwarzenegger and James Cameron to develop the type of fast-paced, violent adventure that has become synonymous with contemporary Hollywood. The development of science fiction hand in hand with computer-generated imagery (CGI) special effects over the next two decades saw the genre become one of the mainstays of the Hollywood global blockbuster system fitting neatly into ancillary markets, specifically video game spin-offs, which in some cases are developed and owned by another arm of the same parent company that owns the film studio.

It is hard now to see science fiction as anything other than a mainstream genre as it has grown to encompass a number of successful film series and sub-genres. In world cinema science fiction hasn't developed to such an extent although there are examples, such as the Australian *Mad Max* (1979–1985) series, Jeunet and Caro's *Delicatessen* (1991) and *The City of Lost Children*, Vincenzo Natali's *Cube* (1997) and Luc Besson's *The Fifth Element* (1997).

Horror

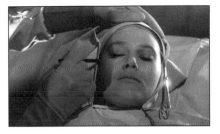

The horror genre grew out of Victorian gothic novels such as Mary Shelley's *Frankenstein* (first published in 1818) and Bram Stoker's *Dracula* (1897). Their European locations and heritage connect them more closely with world cinema than science fiction. The roots of the cinematic style of the Horror film lie in German Expressionism. An early example of this type of film is F. W. Murnau's *Nosferatu* (1922) which features low key lighting, distorted *mise-en-scène*, projected shadows and exaggerated make-up.

The techniques of German silent cinema were imported to Hollywood as many directors sought refuge from Nazism in the 1930s. Universal Studios was closely associated with the development of the horror genre in Hollywood with its stable of stars including Bela Lugosi, Lon Chaney Jr. and Boris Karloff becoming the archetypal Dracula, Wolfman and Frankenstein's Monster respectively. In the 1940s RKO Studios in Hollywood released a series of more psychological horror films produced by Val Lewton, which relied on atmosphere rather than grotesquery; Jacques Tourneur's *Cat People* (1942) is famous for not showing its monster – if indeed it exists at all – but using dark shadows and noises to create suspense.

The stock horror stories of Frankenstein, vampires, werewolves and mummies were taken up by the Hammer studio in London, producing a series of films from the late

1950s through to the early 1970s. These films established the careers of Peter Cushing and Christopher Lee as genre stalwarts. Hammer Films became increasingly tired and exploitative throughout the 1970s as their films began to feature nudity and sex aimed at an adult audience. But as the larger studios began to turn away from the horror genre, Roger Corman began to make low-budget exploitation films in Hollywood, often using the sets and props left over by more mainstream productions. A number of directors and actors started out in Corman's company including Nicolas Roeg and Jack Nicholson (Corman also wrote an interesting article in 1965 entitled 'Surrealism and my Films').

In the 1960s, horror films began to move away from merely depicting 'unnatural' creatures and situations of the type that you might find in folk tales towards a more psychological horror where the threat came from 'ordinary' humans often from within the family. Typical examples used for studying the development of this sub-genre are Alfred Hitchcock's *Psycho* (1960) and Michael Powell's *Peeping Tom* (1960), both of which comment directly on voyeurism and our position as collaborators in the acts committed on screen. Both films allow us to consider misogyny in the horror genre and question the pleasures that we get from watching this type of film. Georges Franju's *Les Yeux sans visage (Eyes Without a Face)* (1960) is a great example of the surreal nature of horror film from this period.

In the 1960s, competition from television and more relaxed censorship led to changes in the target audience for cinema. George A. Romero's films, such as *Night of the Living Dead* (1968), and David Cronenberg's series of body horror films from the 1970s visually develop the ideas initially expressed through vampire films that play on fears of disease and sexuality.

In Italy the 'Giallo' genre had developed out of pulp fiction stories with specifically Italian content. Directors such as Mario Bava and Dario Argento created a series of atmospheric crime and horror films from the 1950s onwards. Argento's films such as *Suspiria* (1977) and *Tenebre* (1982) are seen as classics of the horror 'slasher' genre but also have a distinctly European surreal, gothic atmosphere. In Spain, Jesus Franco developed a reputation for erotic and surreal horror films such as *The Hand of the Dead Man* (1962).

In the 1980s, exploitation films were given a lease of life by the advent of home video systems (hence 'video nasties'). Films such as *Friday the 13th* (1980), *A Nightmare on Elm Street* (1984), *The Evil Dead* (1981) and *Halloween* (1978) spawned ever more ridiculous and self-referential sequels culminating in Wes Craven's deconstruction of the slasher genre, *Scream* (1996).

In recent years the psychological horror film has dominated in Asian cinema with films such as Hideo Nakata's *Ringu* (1998) and Takashi Shimizu's *Ju-on* (2000) successfully crossing over into American and European markets before being re-made in America as *The Ring* (2002) and *The Grudge* (2004), respectively.

The universal appeal of the horror genre and the ways in which it plays on our psychological fears has clear links with the ideas of Surrealism and with psychoanalysis in general. Horror films offer fertile ground to film theorists when discussing issues around spectatorship and representation, some of which we will explore later in this book.

Fantasy

Although the fantasy genre is often seen to include science fiction and horror films, there is also a specific type of fantasy film that is neither horror nor science fiction. These are adventure films, folk tales, fairy stories or the type of sword and sorcery typified by the *Lord of the Rings* trilogy. Fantasy films are set in mythical locations or ancient history where legendary and mythical characters appear. Often fantasy films will draw from a range of religions, ancient traditions or stories and will usually include archetypal characters. Many fantasy films are aimed at a young audience, MGM's *The Wizard of Oz* (1939) being perhaps the best known example from Hollywood's studio period.

In 1940 Britain produced *The Thief of Bagdad*; in France Jean Cocteau directed a version of *Beauty and the Beast; La Belle et la bête* (1946); in Nazi Germany the fantasy film *Münchhausen* (1943) was produced; and in Soviet Russia, Aleksandr Ptushko directed a series of fantasy films with groundbreaking special effects such as *The Stone Flower* (1946) and *Ilya Muromets* (1956). In the 1950s Ray Harryhausen developed stop-frame animation and superimposition special effects techniques that were used for bringing mythological figures to life in a range of fantasy films such as *The 7th Voyage of Sinbad* (1958). These films, based on myths and folk tales, went on to inspire a number of films throughout the 1960s and 1970s that used exotic and dream-like locations to tell stories of princesses and adventurers.

In the 1980s and 1990s, Hollywood produced regular fantasy outings. Although high profile, they were neither particularly popular with critics, nor especially successful financially. John Boorman's *Excalibur* (1981) was described as by Time Out magazine as 'overlong and incoherent – a misguided folly' (Pym, 2005, p. 406). Matthew Robbins' *Dragonslayer* (1981) had lukewarm reviews regardless of its visual panache. Despite his artistic success with *Blade Runner* (1982), Ridley Scott's *Legend* (1985) was said by Philip French in the Observer (Walker, 2000, p. 467) to look like a commercial for soft toilet paper. This type of critical response demonstrates that fantasy films are not often treated seriously as a genre although (or perhaps because) they are popular with a younger audience.

Some of the films from this period were more successful. *The NeverEnding Story* (1984) was made in Germany by Wolfgang Petersen and received good reviews, spawning two sequels. *Wings of Desire* (1987), also made in Germany, by Wim Wenders, can be seen as a fantasy film of a very different type – an arthouse and critical success, re-made in Hollywood as *City of Angels* (1998).

The success of the *Lord of the Rings* trilogy, *The Chronicles of Narnia* (2005) and the *Harry Potter* series of films (2001–present) have, however, led to a renaissance in the fantasy genre, which now marries critical and commercial popularity. These film franchises are ideal for contemporary Hollywood as they run the gamut of opportunities to raise income from ancillary markets such as toys, games and clothing.

Desire and the Spectator

Fantasy films, particularly those with a horror element, use their invented world to depict an expression of our unconscious desires and fears. Many fantasy films deal with issues of sexuality and sexual relations, sometimes metaphorically, sometimes explicitly. Vampires and werewolves are often used as ciphers for male or female predatory sexuality. Other fantasy films can be read as metaphors for sexually transmitted diseases (for example, Cronenberg's 1986 version of *The Fly*), concerns about reproductive technology (*Alien: Resurrection*, 1997) or societal changes in gender relationships (*The Handmaid's Tale*, 1990).

Spectatorship study is an area of Film Studies that has developed since the 1970s out of semiotics, itself a branch of linguistics. In film theory, semiotics was combined with psychoanalysis to consider the relationship between the viewer, seated in the darkened cinema, and the projected image on the screen. The first writers to consider this relationship used the term 'interpellation': this refers to the way that the spectator becomes a subject by being absorbed into the ideology implicit in the film they are watching. This early spectator theory assumes that the film operates on the viewer at a subconscious level – the spectator acts as a child and loses their critical facilities as they are interpellated into the film text. It also assumes that the film has one specific ideology or message, for example a patriarchal or capitalist worldview.

These views have been challenged by subsequent theorists such as Lacan and Mulvey who see the spectator/screen relationship as more complex. Each viewer will simultaneously lose themselves in the film text, while, at the same time, retaining their own personality and critical faculties. This view allows us to see the spectator as someone who makes their own meaning from a film through a combination of different 'readings'.

The film viewer may make a preferred reading: an interpretation that agrees with the ideas and messages that the film-makers intended. Alternatively, the viewer may reject the ideas of the film and make an oppositional reading by disagreeing with the ideology implicit in the text. It is most likely that the film spectator will make a negotiated reading: this will involve the spectator being aware of the messages intended by the film-maker while making their own, independent meaning from the film. As viewers we gain pleasures from watching films, pleasures which involve losing ourselves in a story while simultaneously remaining critical of representations or narrative devices that run contrary to our own experience and world-view.

When applying these spectator theories to fantasy film, we should consider the idea of desire: what desires does viewing a film satisfy and how is desire manifested in the film text? The Surrealists were influenced by the writings of Freud and many fantasy films are ripe for Freudian interpretation or psychoanalysis. Freud's conception of psychoanalysis was a science that could be used to deconstruct the symptoms of his patients in order to uncover the inherent structure of the unconscious. Freud is probably best known for the idea that mental disorder or, more specifically, 'hysteria', is the result of a psychic trauma that has been repressed by the patient. By revealing this repressed memory through therapy, the patient will have a cathartic experience that will 'cure' them. Freud tended to consider that the trauma causing this 'hysteria' was usually of a sexual nature, resulting from repressed sexual fantasies or actual sexual abuse. These ideas can be seen in a number of Hollywood narratives. Alfred Hitchcock's

Spellbound (1945) with its Salvador Dali dream sequence and employment of a Freudian production consultant is a prime example (although its male protagonist and lack of a sexual cause of the trauma are less typically Freudian).

Early surreal and fantasy films can be seen to share this fairly simplistic notion that dream symbols can be used to 'unlock' repressed memories or open the doors of the unconscious (visually represented in a sequence from *Spellbound* where we see a series of doors opening). The power of cinema for the Surrealists was in its ability to access the unconscious of spectators through the process of interpellation: using symbolic imagery to unlock repressed ideas and thereby 'liberate' the viewer from their social conditioning. Their ideas were a relatively naïve combination of Freud, Marx and early montage theories.

Another important theory in psychoanalysis is that of the 'mirror stage', developed by Jacques Lacan (2001, pp. 1–8). This refers to the point at which a young child recognises its own image in the mirror as a representation of itself (separate from its mother) and begins to construct an individual identity based on this image. In Lacan's view, this development of identity based on a reflection is the root cause of self-delusion and narcissism in adults. This idea of self-delusion when confronted by an image can be applied to film theory and would seem to suggest that there is a direct connection between this mirror stage in childhood and the way in which we respond to a cinematic spectacle, deluding ourselves that this representation is reality. This theory offers us a root cause for the desire to look, or 'scopophilia', but also leads to a conflict between the idea of identifying with the characters on screen (narcissism) and voyeuristically desiring the characters.

The development of feminist consideration of these issues in the 1970s led to a concentration on the idea of 'the gaze'; that cinema (particularly Hollywood narrative film) builds on our inherent tendency to voyeurism or scopophilia and offers us a view of the world which is gendered. We are positioned as male spectators with the female body fetishised as an object of male attention and exploitation. The contradiction between the desire to look at, and the need to identify with, an image has been examined by Laura Mulvey. Mulvey (1975, pp. 6–18) argues that the female body in a film is the site of the spectator's desire but is not important to the narrative, the spectator of a conventional narrative film thereby identifies with the male hero who pushes the narrative forward (narcissism) and shares the hero's desire for the female character (voyeurism). When studying fantasy cinema, it is worth considering the representation of male and female characters and how they are positioned in relation to the narrative (how far are they active or passive in developing the narrative – are things done to them or do they do things?). It is also important to ask *who* we are invited to identify with by use of camera angle, editing and *mise-en-scène*.

At this point we should revisit Todorov's definition of the fantastic. In essence, he where three conditions are present:

1. There is a 'hesitation' between reality and the supernatural. The characters in the narrative are uncertain as to whether they are experiencing natural or supernatural events.

2. The spectator experiences a similar uncertainty; they identify with the experience of the character.

3. The spectator will not see the events in the film as allegorical or poetic, but in some way (possibly through identification with the main character) as supposedly real.

If we take this definition on board, we can begin to consider to what extent the films that we are studying match these criteria. We can attempt to identify at what point in the narrative do we leave this zone of 'hesitation' and realise that we are in a supernatural world. Fantasy films tend to occupy the space between reality and unreality; the characters in these films will often look for rational explanations to the strange events that surround them and we, as spectators, will do the same. If we combine these questions with issues of representation and spectatorship, we will have a broad range of tools with which to deconstruct the film texts that we have chosen to study.

3. Surreal Auteurs

Auteur theory is one of the key concepts in Film Studies. Most general Film Studies books will offer a chapter explaining the concept and related debates in depth, so I will discuss these here only briefly. The concept of the *'auteur'* was developed in the late 1950s by a group of French film critics that included André Bazin, François Truffaut and Jean-Luc Godard. They promoted the idea of the film director as being the main creative artist in the process of film production. They identified a difference between the director as *auteur* and the director as *metteur-en-scène* (directors who are competent technicians with no real independent creative identity). An *auteur* was seen as being able to stamp their own personality or signature on a film through use of film language and *mise-en-scène*. *Auteurs* are often associated with genre material through which they are able to develop themes and obsessions particular to themselves.

The following section gives a brief overview of a selection of surreal *auteurs*, including a detailed analysis of one film by each film-maker.

Luis Buñuel (1900–1983)

Buñuel's career spans nearly 50 years and enables us to trace a body of cinematic work directly back to the founders of the Surrealist group. Although they may appear so, his films are not arbitrary; they display a number of key themes and icons that also identify him as an auteur in his own right, outside of the surrealist movement. He is not a comedy director, or a maker of purely absurd or mystical films. All of his films have an element of strangeness about them, as a body of work they offer an almost scientific analysis of human faith and the psyche. They are full of jokes, absurd situations and mystical events yet offer no real solutions. He displays in his films anti-bourgeoisie and anti-religious sentiments yet his films remain both deeply religious and mainly focused on bourgeois concerns. These contradictions make him all the more interesting and give ample scope for investigation into his aims and intentions that, like all good Surrealism, do not match conventional expectations.

Le Fantôme de la liberté / The Phantom of Liberty (1974)

Cast

(selected as there are more than 40 parts)

Adriana Asti:	Prefect of police's Sister
Julien Bertheau:	First Prefect of police
Jean-Claude Brialy:	M. Foucauld
Adolfo Celi:	Doctor Pasolini
Paul Frankeur:	Innkeeper
Michael Lonsdale:	Hatter
Pierre Maguelon:	Gérard, the policeman
François Maistre:	Professor
Hélène Perdrière:	Aunt
Michel Piccoli:	Second Prefect of Police
Claude Piéplu:	Commissioner of Police
Jean Rochefort:	M. Legendre
Bernard Verley:	Judge
Milena Vukotic:	Nurse
Monica Vitti:	Mrs Foucauld

Production Credits

Country:	Italy / France
Language:	French
Producer:	Serge Silberman

Director:	Luis Buñuel
Writers:	Luis Buñuel and
	Jean-Claude Carrière
Cinematography:	Edmond Richard
Editing:	Hélène Plemiannikov

Synopsis

A film in which a series of chance encounters connects a number of disparate, mainly middle class, characters. The story progresses from one situation to the next with no real cause and effect or narrative resolution. It is difficult to summarise as the film intentionally attempts to disrupt the conventions of storytelling.

The film opens in Toledo, Spain in 1808 where Napoleonic troops are carrying out summary executions. The story then moves to contemporary France where some children are given exotic images to look at, their father visits the doctor whose nurse drives to visit her dying father. She stops at a hotel where we meet monks, sadomasochists and incestuous nephews. The nurse leaves the hotel in the morning, giving a professor from the police academy a lift into town. The professor discusses philosophy and social issues with the young recruits, some of whom are later seen stopping a speeding motorist. The motorist visits his doctor where he is told that he has cancer. On returning home he discovers that his daughter has gone missing from school. A sniper is seen randomly killing people from a tower block. The Prefect of police goes to visit his dead sister in a mausoleum; he is arrested and taken back to his office where another Prefect of police takes him out to see the police control a riot at the zoological gardens. The final shot is a close-up of an ostrich's head.

Surrealist and fantasy cinema is a topic that sets itself apart from other such historical studies in its lack of specificity of space and time. As outlined previously, it can be seen that Surrealism has a range of sources and influences; it has developed in a number of locations and times; and it has become associated with some powerful personalities. No discussion of Surrealist cinema can take place without consideration of what Marsha Kinder (1999, p. 2) describes as the 'nomadic discourse' of Luis Buñuel. Although his direct association with the Surrealist movement was limited to his early work in Paris, Buñuel has become the 'representative icon' of Surrealist cinema. He is also an important figure in Spanish cinema, despite spending most of his life in exile. His work can be split into three main stages:

1. Radical Surrealist.

2. The international face of Mexican cinema.

3. French arthouse film-maker.

The Phantom of Liberty was Buñuel's penultimate film, made in this third stage, towards the end of his long career. At the time of production, he was 74 years old and considering retirement. The film summarises many of the concerns that permeate his work and was one of his own favourites:

'Chance governs all things; necessity, which is far from having the same purity, comes only later. If I have a soft spot for any one of my movies, it would be for The Phantom of Liberty, *because* it tries to work out just this theme.' (Buñuel, 1984, p. 171)

The film contains short incidents and scenarios collected from throughout Buñuel's life, arranged in the style of a surreal game where seemingly disconnected ideas are linked by chance encounters.

The film opens in Toledo where the Napoleonic army are about to execute a group of men who cry out 'down with liberty!' (apparently based on an historical event). Toledo was the city that so impressed the young Buñuel in 1923 that he founded a pseudo secret society named 'The Order of Toledo' for his friends, including the young artist Salvador Dali and the poet Federico Garcia Lorca.

The disconnected narrative of The Phantom of Liberty revisits the ideas of Buñuel's directorial debut *Un chien andalou*, a short (17 minute) Surrealist film, based on the logic of dreams. *Un chien andalou* appears to be a love story with images that were intended to be irrational (according to Buñuel, any sequences that could have a rational explanation were removed at the scriptwriting stage). This early film shows the influence of Expressionist cinematic style and is still powerful today, particularly the opening sequence in which an eye is sliced with a razor blade. The influence of the Surrealist movement is also evident: firstly, in its focus on dreams and the unconscious; secondly, in the method of its narrative construction – created through the play of associations between two men suggesting 'random' scenes to each other; and thirdly, in its deconstruction of a popular genre (the romantic melodrama).

The Phantom of Liberty continues to demonstrate Buñuel's early Surrealist roots but is also infused with biographical details. When he was a student in Madrid, he had seen a dead woman's hair 'growing' from a tomb in the moonlight. The sight made a strong impression on him and he used the image in this film some 50 years later. In the 1940s, when he lived in Los Angeles but had no prospects of film work, he wrote down the idea about a missing girl whose parents fruitlessly search for her while she is beside them; invisible and yet not invisible. When the Carmelite monk says 'If everyone prayed every day to Saint Joseph, everything would be fine', this was a quote that had stuck with Buñuel when he was visiting a monastery in the 1960s. One of the most poignant biographical details used in *The Phantom of Liberty* is the sequence when the doctor tries to avoid telling his patient that he has cancer of the liver. This was based on Buñuel's experience of being told that he had a cyst on his liver (he died of cancer of the liver in 1983).

The title of the film is a homage to Karl Marx and Friederich Engel's *Communist Manifesto*, specifically this quote of the opening sentence, 'A spectre is haunting Europe–the spectre of Communism' (in French, spectre is translated as *fantôme*). Buñuel explains this link with the *Communist Manifesto* in 'Objects of Desire: Conversations with Luis Buñuel', extracts from which are published in the booklet that accompanies the Criterion DVD release of *The Phantom of Liberty*. He also mentions it in his autobiography (see Bunuel, 1984, p. 249). This sentence refers to the way in which the idea of communism was being used pejoratively by the authorities in the late nineteenth century to attack all political parties opposed to the established order (church, aristocracy and state). *The Communist Manifesto* was written to offer a positive vision of the views, aims and tendencies of communists from across Europe. Buñuel and the Surrealists were closely linked to the communists in the 1930s but by the 1950s Buñuel had developed an antipathy towards the party.

The title of *The Phantom of Liberty* is also taken from a line of dialogue from his 1969 film *The Milky Way* 'my liberty is only a phantom'; possibly referring to the way in which the civil rights movements of the 1960s had been seen as a threat to the established order – the 'phantom' of radical liberal ideas 'haunting' capitalist society. It is more likely to refer to the illusive nature of freedom, to the ways in which our destinies are controlled by chance or, as Buñuel would have it:

'we so often find ourselves at complicated crossroads which lead to other crossroads, to ever more fantastic labyrinths. Somehow we must choose a path.' (Buñuel, 1984, p. 171)

This quote not only parallels the structure of the film but also summarises Buñuel's philosophy of life. After being awarded an Oscar for best foreign language film in the previous year (for *The Discreet Charm of the Bourgeoisie*, 1972) he appears to have regained the creative autonomy of his earlier films. *The Phantom of Liberty* can therefore be seen as a personal film from a director reflecting back on a long creative career.

Narrative Structure, Characters and Themes

The Phantom of Liberty is a film that celebrates the notion of chance encounters and takes this concept to 'wage war' on the very idea of storytelling. The overall structure of the film is one of seemingly unconnected episodes linked together by random encounters. The story is passed from one scene to the next as if the narrative is a relay race: the narrative 'baton' is passed on by means of a minor character from one scene becoming the next major character. When watching a film, we usually expect the various interlocking narratives to be revisited and the film to end with a clear resolution to each story. In this film, we are left wondering what will happen in each section and most of the characters do not reappear. As mentioned earlier, a number of the scenes in the film are taken from Buñuel's own experience and structured using the Surrealist notion of automatism or stream of consciousness, where ideas are allowed to develop without the control of reason or aesthetics.

Buñuel (1985, p. 249) outlines the film's themes in his autobiography as being the following:

1. The search for truth and the need to abandon the truth as soon as you have found it.

2. The implacable nature of social rituals.

3. The importance of coincidence.

4. The importance of personal morality.

5. The essential mystery of all things.

It is worth considering where and how these themes are illustrated in this and some of Buñuel's other films.

1. The search for truth and the need to abandon the truth as soon as you have found it

This theme is evident in the narrative structure of *The*

Phantom of Liberty. As one search for truth is succeeded by another, we begin to realise that the film is an attack on conventional storytelling that attempts to offer truth through a coherent, logical narrative universe. Buñuel's personal search for truth led to his association with and rejection of organisations as diverse as the Catholic Church, Parisian Surrealism and the Communist Party. The Parisian Surrealists created rules and manifestos that mocked the idea of universal truths while paradoxically offering a new utopia through Surrealist techniques. Buñuel was not afraid to rebel against the strictures of established organisations as he saw their relativism along with their social and historical nature.

In *The Phantom of Liberty* characters are searching for truth: Monsieur Legrende (Jean Rochefort) is attempting to find out if he has cancer and whether his daughter is missing; when he discovers the answers to these questions, he loses interest in them. The viewer is also attempting to make sense of the 'truth' within the story.

2. The implacable nature of social rituals

The Parisian Surrealists were interested in the idea of deconstructing social rituals and using them to 'liberate the subconscious'. *The Phantom of Liberty* is structured around a series of social rituals. Formal introductions and conversations are used as transitions between apparently disconnected sequences. Buñuel plays with social conventions by turning them on their head yet retains their superficial formality. Scenes are played straight with a comic intent that is never realised in laughter or slapstick. The film features social rituals such as Monsieur Legrende's visit to the doctor, the formal lecture at the police academy and the sniper's court case. The microcosm of the provincial hotel is used to present a range of implacable rituals from the small talk between the patron and his guests to the Hatter's drinks party that starts as a formal affair but disintegrates when he starts to be masochistically flagellated by his assistant.

The most obvious attempt to expose the relative nature of social customs is the dinner party scene where the social acceptability of defecation and eating is reversed. In this scene the guests are seated around the table on flushing toilets. They politely discuss various issues around the topic of defecation whilst publicly using the toilets that they are sitting on. When a guest is hungry, he excuses himself and retires to a private cubicle to eat food. This use of the dinner party metaphor had been fully developed in Buñuel's previous film. *The Discreet Charm of the Bourgeoisie* follows a group of middle class friends through a series of comic and surreal sketches in which they never quite manage to sit down and eat a meal together; yet all the time they maintain their ability to observe social conventions.

3. The importance of coincidence

Chance encounters have been used as a means by which to create Dada and Surrealist art from artworks such as Hans Arp's series of collages 'Arranged According to the Laws of Chance' (1917) to David Lynch's use of chance occurrences to develop scripts and create characters. These experiments can be seen to prefigure or parallel the way that scientific ideas such as chaos theory are used as devices to develop contemporary cinematic narratives. Classical Hollywood attempts to hide coincidence in narrative through conventions that are often ridiculed by cineastes and makers of parodies. *The Naked Gun* (1988, 1991, 1994) and *Airplane!* (1980, 1982) film franchises play with these conventions (as does Mel Brooks in comedies such as *Spaceballs* (1987) and *Robin Hood Men in Tights* (1993)). You can also find websites devoted to Hollywood clichés, where the artificial nature of Hollywood plot devices is expounded (www.moviecliches.com is one example).

In *The Phantom of Liberty* coincidence takes centre stage as the story shifts its focus from one chance encounter to the next. The characters in the film, of which there are more than 40 credited, are taken from a range of middle class 'types'. The characters are not particularly allowed to develop as personalities; they are more like a series of fairly sympathetic stereotypes that represent institutions and professions as diverse as religious orders, doctors, nurses, the police, the military and the teaching profession. Each character appears to be subject to coincidence and have no control over their fate.

4. The importance of personal morality

The Phantom of Liberty depicts characters who may hold a range of personal moral viewpoints but their situations appear to be the consequence of the social rituals, laws and morality that the Professor (François Maistre) discusses at the police academy. He gives a lecture to a class of delinquent policemen on this subject which is constantly interrupted until only two officers are left in the class. The professor continues, using a dinner party at his friend's house to illustrate a point he is making. In its suggestion of various sexual transgressions, the film emphasises how the concept of morality is a personal issue. This theme, the analysis of morality and the deconstruction of formal religious strictures, is most successfully illustrated by Buñuel in his 1969 film *The Milky Way*. This film uses quotes from historical Catholic texts to construct a view of muddled Christian morality that would make any personal set of moral strictures seem reasonable in comparison.

5. The essential mystery of all things

In classical Hollywood narratives such as Hitchcock's *North by Northwest* (1959), a case of mistaken identity is used to set off a chain of events that, to the protagonist, appear a tumultuous pattern of coincidences or conspiracies. The events are gradually revealed to the spectator to have a meaning and the mystery is solved; there is a pattern that is fully explained to both the spectator and the protagonist. In Buñuel's film, there is no such reassurance; the mysteries remain mysterious, yet the characters in the film seem fairly content to live in an essentially mysterious world. As spectators, we are put in the position of the classical cinematic 'wrong man' – we feel that we are involved in a sequence of events to which there should be an answer, that there is a Freudian code or key that will unlock the meaning of the film. Essentially *The Phantom of Liberty* reminds us that we are not in control of our destinies and that there are no answers. This disjointed and self-reflective response is at the heart of Surrealist art and film-making; perhaps this is why surreal cinema is a term that cannot be tied down to a specific temporal or geographical location.

Film Style

Renowned for his ability to work to tight budgets and schedules (after his experiences of working in the Mexican film industry), Buñuel was more concerned with constructing ideas than building complex sets or ostentatiously flaunting a cinematic style. One example of his economic style is the scene where the Prefect of Police receives a telephone call from his dead sister; we don't have to see the corpse reach out from the coffin – it is easier to show the telephone (a cheap prop), and allow our imaginations to construct the scenario. It is also interesting to note the absence of a musical score in the soundtrack. Instead, subtle sound effects (for which Buñuel is credited) are used to create atmosphere. One example of this is the riot at the end of the film, suggested only by the sound effects. Contrast this with Bernardo Bertolucci's reconstruction of the 1968 Parisian riots in *The Dreamers* (2003); expensive to stage, involving the use of a large cast and crew and closing down Parisian streets.

Buñuel's Themes and Obsessions

It is worth looking at each director's work for common themes and obsessions. These can be seen as an *auteur* signature and allow us to identify connections between what may seem a disparate group of films. In Buñuel's work there are themes that reflect the main concerns of the Surrealists, and there are also personal themes and obsessions that have grown out of Buñuel's own experience.

Dreams and the subconscious

Many of his films contain dream or fantasy sequences; the fantasy is rarely overtly weird or fantastic, tending more towards the personal, internal fantasy. Other films have no clear delineation between the worlds of personal fantasy and reality, a dream-like atmosphere pervades the narrative and we are never sure whether we are viewing reality or a dreamed experience.

Eroticism and fetishism

Buñuel had the reputation of being a sadist with a taste for sexual violence. In his films we often see drugged or hypnotised women; his female protagonists are seduced by older men in positions of power. Buñuel is also reputed to have had a fetish for women's feet and high-heeled shoes. There is regular use of close-up shots of women's legs and feet in his films.

Religion

Religious themes recur in nearly all of his films. We see priests and nuns treated with irreverence.We also see a host of religious symbolism; crucifixes, religious robes and religious ceremonies (weddings and funerals).

Voyeurism

In Buñuel's films, characters are often peering through keyholes or around doors. Characters view the world through windows and bars, and as viewers we are often implicated in this voyeurism.

The body

Physical disabilities feature in many of Buñuel's films; artificial limbs, crutches and facial disfigurement may be central to the narrative or appear as secondary elements. The camera often dwells on close-ups of hands and feet. There are severed hands in *Un chien andalou* and *The Exterminating Angel* (1962), and in *Tristana* (1970) the main character has an artificial leg.

Birds and beasts

Buñuel studied entomology and insects often appear in his films from the moth and ants in *Un chien andalou* to the cockroaches in *The Discreet Charm of the Bourgeoisie*. A range of other animals appear in his films, often in unusual situations: dead donkeys in pianos (*Un chien andalou*); cows in bedrooms (*L'Âge d'Or*); a bear and sheep in the dining room (*The Exterminating Angel*).

Everyday objects and activities

These are often imbued with a mystical or reverential quality. We often see characters eating fruit, playing the piano or sewing. Mysterious boxes appear in his films from the striped box in *Un chien andalou* to the box belonging to an oriental customer in *Belle de jour* (1967).

Analysis of a short sequence from *The Phantom of Liberty*

Below is an analysis of a short sequence from *The Phantom of Liberty* that illustrates some of Buñuel's themes and stylistic approaches. The sequence is approximately 9 minutes long and contains three scenarios featuring the character of Monsieur Foucauld. The sequence is from early on in the film; it starts at approximately 8 minutes and ends at 17 minutes (Chapter 3 of the Criterion DVD release).

The sequence begins with a close-up of a spider in a frame, a reference to Buñuel's interest in entomology. Monsieur Foucauld is sitting in a French middle class apartment, the mise-en-scène is impersonal, grey and muted; the furniture and décor are not dissimilar from the interiors in films from any one of Buñuel's three periods: the apartment in *Un chien andalou*, the Mexican colonial interiors of *The Exterminating Angel* or Severine's home in *Belle de jour* all have the same bourgeoise décor, interiors that signify the genre of melodrama. Monsieur Foucauld comments on the symmetry of the neatly organised apartment and places the framed spider on the mantelpiece as if to symbolically disrupt the equilibrium. These opening shots are disconcerting to the viewer who will attempt to construct some logical meaning from them. Madame Foucauld (Monica Vitti) enters the room looking beautiful in her designer dress. Her husband appears confused, as they begin to converse; the dialogue is slightly uneasy as if the two characters are drifting through the social rituals of married life without being aware of each other. Their first exchange demonstrates that the characters are as uncertain as we are as to the nature of the sequence; the husband asks:

> `'Are you back already?'`

To which she responds:

> `'What do you mean? I never went out.'`

The dialogue, matched with the way that they are avoiding each other's gaze, hints at hidden tensions. She seems to offer an explanation for this mood – perhaps he is tired? She suggests that they should go to the sea for a week, instead of taking up her offer he again presents us with a riddle:

> `'But why the sea? The sea is no`
> `longer the sea.'`

Again the audience is puzzled by the actions on screen. The scene is shot in a removed, economical style with the viewer positioned as if they were the audience of a stage production through the use of few edits and mainly mid to long shots. The camera unobtrusively pans and tracks to follow the theatrical dialogue. Madame Foucauld says that she has passed him in the street and he hadn't even recognised her. He replies by introducing the theme of dream and sleep – the uncertainty that occurs as you lie in bed waiting for sleep (the Surrealists were very interested in these *hypnagogic* experiences – the kind of vivid dream-like experiences that occur as you are falling asleep), in mentioning his inability to sleep, he is pre-empting the subsequent nocturnal scene.

In his later films, Buñuel personified the new, *auteur*-based, confidence of European cinema. Despite describing actors as 'cockroaches', much of his later success relied on his ability to call upon established acting talent such as Michel Piccoli. Madame Foucauld is played by Monica Vitti, star of European films such as Michelangelo Antonioni's *L'Avventura* (1960), which also dissects the attitudes and relationships of the idle upper middle class. Jean-Claude Brialy (Monsieur Foucauld) was a friend of French New Wave luminaries Jacques Rivette and Jean-Luc Godard.

The Foucauld's nanny returns with their daughter, who has been given photographs by a stranger in the park. As the married couple view these photographs, their passions are aroused. The images are initially hidden from us but as we are subsequently given a privileged, voyeuristic viewpoint, we see that the pictures are those of buildings. In these images, Buñuel takes a swipe at some of his signature targets: the Arc de Triomphe, symbol of French nationalism, is called 'indecent'. The established church is mocked as the image of the Sacré Coeur is torn in half and described as 'going too far'. In a surreal twist, these 'shocking' images are then given back to the daughter as if they are now harmless. The nanny is dismissed, despite the apparent benign nature of the images. Social relations are critiqued in their bourgeois condescension towards their domestic employee. When the daughter is given the pictures back, she asks if she can trade them for pictures of spiders. This refers back to the opening shot of the sequence but rather than clarifying the earlier symbolism, it makes it more obscure (or perhaps more personal as the child's discussion about spiders with her father refers to

Buñuel's study of entomology).

The next scene again opens with a close-up, this time an alarm clock being set at 10.30pm is artificially framed. The camera moves from an extreme close-up of the clock, out to a wide shot of the bed and back again with no edits – a church clock strikes one o'clock in the distance and hours have passed in a few seconds. The sequence shows Monsieur Foucauld involved in a disturbed nights sleep: as the hours skip past, there are strange symbolic visitations to his bedroom; a postman, a cockerel, a dark lady with a candle and an ostrich all walk past the end of his bed as if his bedroom is a stage (the ostrich anticipates the final shot of the film – an ostrich's eye in extreme close-up). Here we have Surrealist clichés: the clock, the dream, Freudian symbolism. As viewers we are not sure if this is a dream sequence – the character appears to be fully conscious as time keeps skipping one hour after the other. The scene cuts to a new location as Monsieur Foucauld is finishing a consultation with his doctor who dismisses psychoanalysis:

> 'If you want to discuss your dreams, see a psychoanalyst. He'll listen to you for months, years if you want to.'

Buñuel appears to be dismissing the ideas that are often credited as a major influence on the development of Surrealism. He always had a healthy cynicism about psychoanalysis, saying in his biography 'psychoanalysis [is] severely limited, a form of therapy reserved for the upper classes' (Buñuel, 1983, p. 175). As if to answer these criticisms, Monsieur Foucauld produces evidence in the form of a physical letter from the nocturnal postman. Before we can hear what is in the letter, however, a nurse enters the room and the narrative focus shifts to her story.

This sequence illustrates the narrative dynamic of the film whilst also containing elements of Surrealism and Buñuel's auteur signature. The film style is economic and almost theatrical, with minimal camera movements or editing. For example, when Monsieur Foucauld consults the doctor and the nurse enters the room at the end of this sequence, three characters and their dilemmas are presented to us:

1. The doctor is reading the letter, engaged in the contents of the mysterious letter.

2. Foucauld contemplates the doctor's response.

3. The nurse enters the room and asks for the doctor's attention.

All of this is covered by one developing shot with no edits, in the style of a B-movie or television melodrama. Sound is used sparingly in this sequence, with no music or non-diegetic sound, emphasis given to sound effects such as the clock's ticking or the bird's footsteps.

The locations are sparsely and neatly organised with the props and costumes of bourgeoise lifestyle: antiques, books, panelled interiors, designer dresses and three-piece suits. Social structures are delineated in the relationships between the family and their maid, the doctor and his patient, the husband and wife. With its emphasis on the dream and symbolism, this sequence clearly illustrates some of the major concerns of Buñuel and Surrealism.

Critical Views

'The Phantom of Liberty is a patchwork of comedic sketches

and sight gags through which Buñuel ravages a complacent European culture and summons the various sexual hang-ups and historical and cultural disconnections of his characters. This heady masterwork isn't particularly easy to decipher, but it's best approached as the literal comedy of manners Buñuel intends it to be.' (Gonzalez, 2003 *Slant Magazine*).

'*The Phantom of Liberty* may very well be the most accomplished, ambitious and Surrealist work of his 54-year film career. Indeed, this is a film that comprehensively challenges traditional narrative conventions. At the same time, the film deals with a variety of transgressive subjects and presents an intense criticism against established social institutions. It is a complex, paradoxical, subversive and radical film, which has promoted endless debates and encouraged a variety of readings.' (Lanzagorta, 2002 *Senses of Cinema*).

Filmography

The later European co-productions

Cet obscur objet du désir (That Obscure Object of Desire) (1977)

Le Fantôme de la liberté (The Phantom of Liberty) (1974)

Le Charme discret de la bourgeoisie (The Discreet Charm of the Bourgeoisie) (1972)

Tristana (1970)

La Voie lactée (The Milky Way) (1969)

Belle de jour (1967)

Le Journal d'une femme de chambre (The Diary of a Chambermaid) (1964)

Viridiana (1961)

The Mexican cycle

Simón del desierto (Simon of the Desert) (1965)

El Ángel exterminador (The Exterminating Angel) (1962)

La Joven (The Young One) (1960)

La Fièvre monte à El Pao (1959)

Nazarín (1959)

La Mort en ce jardin (1956)

Cela s'appelle l'aurore (1956)

El Río y la muerte (1955)

Ensayo de un crimen (The Criminal Life of Archibaldo de la Cruz) (1955)

Las Aventuras de Robinson Crusoe (The Adventures of Robinson Crusoe) (1954)

Abismos de pasión (Wuthering Heights) (1954)

La Ilusión viaja en tranvía (1954)

El (This Strange Passion) (1953)

El Bruto (The Brute) (1953)

Una Mujer sin amor (A Woman Without Love) (1952)

Subida al cielo (1952)

La Hija del Engaño (1951)

Susana (1951)

Los Olvidados (The Young and the Damned) (1950)

El Gran Calavera (1949)

Gran Casino (1947)

Early films

Las Hurdes (Land Without Bread) (1933)

L'Âge d'or (1930)

Un chien andalou (1929)

Luis Buñuel on Surrealist Cinema (1953)

'Hence it is agreed that the theme [of this lecture] shall be "The Cinema as Artistic Expression", or more concretely, as an instrument of poetry, with all that that word can imply of the sense of liberation, of subversion of reality, of the threshold of the marvellous world of the subconscious, of non-conformity with the limited society that surrounds us...

... I will give a concrete example, the film called *Detective Story*. The structure of its subject is perfect, the director excellent, the actors extraordinary, the realisation brilliant, etc. but all this talent, all this ability, all the complications which the making of a film involve, have been put at the service of an idiotic story, of a remarkable moral wretchedness. This reminds me of the extraordinary machine of *Ôpus II*, a vast machine made of the best steel, with a thousand complex gears, with tubes, manometers, dials precise as a watch, as big as a liner, whose sole use was to gum postage stamps...

...The cinema is a magnificent and perilous weapon when wielded by a free spirit. It is the best instrument to express the world of dreams, of emotions, of instinct. The creative mechanismof cinema images through its manner of functioning, is among all the means of human expression the one which comes nearest to the mind of man, or, even more, which best imitates the functioning of the mind in the state of dreaming... Then begins, on the screen and within the man, the incursion into the night of the unconscious, the images, as in dream, appear and disappear through 'dissolves' and fadeouts; time and space become flexible, retrace or extend at will, chronological order and relative values of duration no longer reality; cyclic action is accomplished in a few minutes or in several centuries, movements accelerate their speed...

... I take for mine the words of Engels, who defined the function of the novelist (understood in this case as that of film maker): The novelist will have accomplished his task honourably when, through a faithful depiction of authentic social relations, he will have destroyed the conventional representation of the nature of these relations, shaken the optimism of the bourgeois world and obliged the reader to question the permanence of the existing order, even if he does not directly propose a conclusion to us, even if he does not openly take sides.' (extract from Buñuel in Fowler (ed.), 2002 pp. 45–8)

Jean Cocteau and *Orphée (Orpheus)* (1950)

Jean Cocteau (1889–1963)

Cast

Jean Marais:	Orphee
François Périer:	Heurtebise
María Casares:	The Princess
Marie Déa:	Eurydice
Henri Crémieux:	The Man
Juliette Gréco:	Aglaonice
Roger Blin:	Writer
Edouard Dermithe:	Cégeste
Maurice Carnege:	Judge
René Worms:	Judge
Pierre Bertin:	The Inspector
Jacques Varennes:	First Judge
Jean Cocteau:	Narrator
Renée Cosima:	Bacchante
Jean-Pierre Melville:	Hotel Manager
Jean-Pierre Mocky:	Un poète

Production Credits

Country:	France

Language:	French
Producer:	André Paulvé
Director:	Jean Cocteau
Writers:	Jean Cocteau
Cinematography:	Nicolas Hayer
Editing:	Jacqueline Sadoul
Music:	Georges Auric

Jean Cocteau was born into a wealthy bourgeois family and by the age of 19 he had published poetry and was the editor of a literary magazine. He became well known among Parisian intellectuals and, with their support, he performed 'absurdist' poems to live audiences. In 1909, at the age of 20, he met Sergei Diaghilev, director of the Ballet Russes and went on to work on the controversial ballet 'Parade' with Pablo Picasso and the composer Eric Satie. He stayed in Nazi-occupied France during the Second World War, initially seeming to support the Nazis; he renewed his friendships with radical artists as the Germans began to lose the war.

He became an important cultural figure within France, particularly known for his poetry. He developed these poetic ideas into the limited number of films that he made. Despite (or perhaps because of) their personal and literary roots, his films are seen as important texts in the history of cinema. Cocteau wrote a manifesto on film and was a member of a number of international film academies.

Synopsis

Cocteau's *Orphée* is a re-telling of the Greek myth of Orpheus, set in contemporary post-war Paris. The story involves the famous poet Orpheus, who falls in love with the mysterious Princess. His wife (Eurydice) is taken by the Princess (who represents Death) and Orpheus has to descend to a strange underworld realm in order to save her. He is accompanied by Heurtebise (the Princess's assistant) and, when there, has to decide whether he loves the Princess or Eurydice. He is allowed to return with Eurydice on the condition that he does not look upon her. Unfortunately, he sees her in the rear view mirror of a car and she vanishes. Orpheus is attacked and killed by an angry mob, the Princess allows him to be reunited with Eurydice and they find themselves back at home in their bedroom with no memory of the strange events.

Jean Cocteau was a French film-maker, playwright, artist, novelist and poet who was involved with a range of important twentieth century literary and art movements. His name may be known to contemporary audiences as one of the fictional Grand Masters of the secretive 'Priory of Sion' in Dan Brown's novel *The Da Vinci Code*. Unlike the other *auteurs* discussed here, Cocteau is as famous for his other artistic endeavours as he is for his film work.

Cocteau mixed in the revolutionary modernist artistic circles of Paris between the wars. He developed friendships with painters such as Matisse and Braque as well as composers such as Igor Stravinsky. Surrealism was born in this environment where there was a synergy created by the meeting of ideas across a range of disciplines. It is interesting to see how high art forms such as painting, ballet, classical music and opera became the arena of debate on issues of political change, artistic form and the meaning of modernity. The aristocracy were present at these modernist events, as were the artisans from the poorer areas of Paris. In this atmosphere, the artistic merit of films was more important than their commercial value; films were made to experiment with form and provoke a response rather than to reach and entertain a large audience.

Unlike the eternal exile Buñuel, Cocteau was very much a part of Parisian and French culture throughout his life. His political views were also very different to Buñuel and his reputation suffered from his decision to stay in Nazi-occupied France. He was seen to be sympathetic towards the Nazi cause; this may have been pragmatism but the damage to his image can be seen reflected in the character of *Orphée* who is becoming less relevant in the post-Holocaust world.

The young Cocteau was present at the premiere of *Un chien andalou* in 1929. The following year, Cocteau produced his first film after obtaining funding from the aristocratic Vicomte de Noailles (who also financially supported Buñuel and Dali's *L'Âge d'Or* in the same year). This independent finance allowed Cocteau to make a very personal film, *Le Sang d'un poète* (*Blood of a Poet*, 1930), with which he developed his own mythological and poetic vision in cinematic form. The film was wrongly aligned with the scandal of *L'Âge d'Or* and with the developing Surrealist movement due to their common commissioner and their almost simultaneous appearance. But *Le Sang d'un poète* was not intended to be a Surrealist film. Cocteau avoided direct symbolism or dream imagery, preferring a more allegorical or poetic approach to the construction of meaning. The film tells the story of a poet who is condemned to walk the corridors of a strange purgatory hotel. This theme can be seen repeated in other European arthouse films such as Bergman's *The Silence* (1963) and Resnais's *Last Year in Marienbad* (1961) or even in recent Hollywood studies of alienation such as Sofia Coppola's *Lost in Translation* (2003).

After the Second World War and a second recovery from opium addiction, Cocteau returned to film-making with his adaptation of the fairy tale, *La Belle et la bête (Beauty and the Beast,* 1946). The film stars Cocteau's intimate friend, Jean Marais, and is a visually stunning period piece with a fairly conventional fantasy narrative.Following the success of *La Belle et la bête*, Cocteau proceeded to make more conventional films such as *L'Aigle à deux têtes* (1948) and *Les Parents terribles* (1948). In 1950, he worked with Jean-Pierre Melville on a film adaptation of his play *Les Enfants terribles*. Melville was a model for the French New Wave directors such as Truffaut and Godard, and he also appeared as an actor in Cocteau's next film *Orphée (Orpheus)* (1950).

Sitting between the realism of the nascent French New Wave movement and the fantasy of *La Belle et la bête*, *Orphée* updates the Greek legend of Orpheus to contemporary post-war Paris. The film again stars Jean Marais and is the second film in his highly personal Orphic Trilogy. In 1960, he made his last film, *Le Testament d'Orphée (Testament of Orpheus)*. This final film in the trilogy elaborates the ideas of his previous films and reflects upon the poetic function of cinema as well as Cocteau's own life and art.

Historical and Social Context

Orphée was made before the birth of the French 'New Wave' movement and occupies the ground between fantasy and realism. It was produced shortly after the Second World War, and the effects of the war on Cocteau and Paris can be seen represented in the narrative and the *mise-en-scène*: the mysterious radio messages are similar to the coded broadcasts aimed at the French resistance during the war; the courtroom scenes are reminiscent of wartime interrogations. Cocteau uses exteriors of bombed-out factories and buildings to represent purgatory; their interiors are used to stage the afterlife. It is interesting to compare Cocteau's vision with Powell and Pressburger's heaven in *A Matter of Life and Death* (1946). One vision is organised and utopian; the other is apocalyptic and conspiratorial.

Orphée moved away from the more experimental style of *Le Sang d'un poète*, using elements of popular genres in the same way that Buñuel was also to do. On a more personal level, Cocteau was aware that his poetic work was no longer as fashionable and he mocks avant-garde poetry which he shows a publication entitled 'Nudisme', the pages of which are completely blank. Orpheus thinks that this is absurd; his friend ('The Man') responds that it is 'less absurd than if it were full of absurd writing'. The character of Jacques Cégeste, a promising poet who is cut down in his prime, can be seen to parallel the death of Cocteau's friend Raymond Radiguet. Radiguet was a controversial young writer and close friend of Cocteau (it was rumoured that they were lovers) who died at the age of 20 from typhoid fever; his death stunned the literary world and had a profound effect on Cocteau. When 'The Man' in the café tells Orpheus to 'astonish us', this is a direct reference to the time when Cocteau was famously told by Diaghilev 30 years earlier to 'Etonne-moi!'

Narrative Structure, Genre and Style

Orphée is the second of Cocteau's Orphic Trilogy and is the film that most closely follows the original myth. In this regard it has a fairly conventional mythological narrative. There is an established equilibrium at the café, followed by a disruption of equilibrium caused by the death of Cégeste and his encounter with the Princess. Orpheus is then thrown into a fantasy world and the film finishes with a new equilibrium.

The film takes this conventional narrative and plays with our expectations, subtly shifting from one genre to another. The opening sequence could almost be a realist film from the French 'New Wave'; it then moves into what appears to be a horror scenario with Death living in a mysterious mansion. The scenes at home with Eurydice are played out like a melodrama or soap opera but mutate into a fantasy journey using Cocteau's techniques of backward filming and tilted cameras as they descend to the underworld. The underworld courtroom scene has the feel of a wartime drama and makes reference to Gestapo interrogations. Comedic elements are introduced as Orpheus farcically tries to avoid looking at Eurydice. This comedy is subtly emphasised by the use of props such as the rubber gloves to enter the kingdom of death, the fetishised 'Sirens' in their leather jackets and knowing self-mockery involving a portrait of the suffering artist/poet.

The film is not an overtly Surrealist project, although it does have surreal themes and episodes. It seems to better fit the definition of a fantasy film, meeting Todorov's first two conditions of 'the fantastic' (Gelder, 2000, p. 19):

1. Orpheus is uncertain as to whether he is imagining the events, the mirror acting as a boundary between the natural and the supernatural, sleeping and dreaming.

2. We, as spectators, are not sure whether the events are supernatural. It appears to be confirmed when the Princess visits Orpheus through the mirror and when Heurtebise vanishes and re-appears.

Todorov's third condition, that the events are real to the character in the film, is possibly not met. Due to the poetic nature of the film's protagonist, we are not sure whether the events are merely created by Orpheus's imagination. We are therefore able to interpret the film as an allegory; alternatively the location shooting and references to contemporary life could lead us to see the film as a 'real' event. The meaning made from the film will depend on, among other things, our knowledge of the film's context and Cocteau's other work. These opportunities for multiple, personal readings of the film, offer us an interesting area of debate around the film text.

Cocteau's Themes and Obsessions

Cocteau saw all of the arts as interconnected. He said of *Testament of Orpheus* (1960): 'This film may be the first attempt at transmuting words into acts, at organising these acts instead of organising the words of a poem, a syntax of images instead of a story accompanied by words' (from an essay by Cocteau published in the notes accompanying the Criterion DVD release of the Orphic Trilogy). He saw himself foremost as a poet, conscious of his own authorial power; he was destined to make very personal films which have been variously accused of self-indulgence and pretension. But despite the self-referential nature of much of his work, there is no denying the powerful lyricism of his cinematic images and the importance of Cocteau to twentieth century visual and literary culture.

Death

Death, resurrection, the afterlife and rebirth are all themes that are developed through his work. He was interested in the mythological phoenix who dies only to be reborn from its ashes; the flower that is destroyed and rebuilt in *Le Testament d'Orphée* is one example of this symbolism.

71

Poetry

Cocteau used films as 'poetic vehicles'. His works, particularly the Orphic Trilogy, reflect on the role of the poet in society and in the world. The figure of the poet is more important in French society than in the UK. In French schools classic poetry is learnt by heart and there are a number of regular television programmes about literature. The French state supports literature through the Institut de France and the Académie Française, helping poetry to have a higher profile within French society.

Mirrors

The symbolic power of the mirror is used in nearly all of Cocteau's films. Mirrors are gateways to other worlds, the means by which we see our own death and develop our sense of identity. Cocteau wrote: 'We watch ourselves grow old in mirrors. They bring us closer to death' (from an essay reprinted in the notes accompanying the Criterion DVD release of the Orphic Trilogy).

The sea

The primal power of the sea, its ability to destroy and give birth, appears in his work.

Special effects

Cocteau utilised and developed a range of special effects to create his fantasy worlds. Reverse filming, superimposition and tilted camera angles are used extensively.

Mythology

Some of his films are based on ancient myths and fairy tales such as Beauty and the Beast and Orpheus. Cocteau also developed his own personal mythology, which in some ways actively helped to market his own celebrity status (in a more subtle version of Salvador Dali's renowned self-publicity).

Casting

Cocteau would cast his friends and lovers in his films, some were professional actors but many were not. His films feature cameos from stars such as Yul Brynner, directors such as Jean-Pierre Melville and artists such as Pablo Picasso.

Analysis of a short sequence from *Orphée*

Below is an analysis of a short sequence from *Orphée* that illustrates some of Cocteau's trademarks and the relationship of his work to Surrealism and fantasy cinema. The sequence is approximately 8 minutes long, during which Heurtebise reveals the true nature of 'The Princess' and takes Orpheus into the realm of death. The sequence starts at approximately 52 minutes and ends at 60 minutes.

The sequence starts as Heurtebise summons Orpheus to his bedroom with the news that Eurydice is dead. The shot of Heurtebise is framed with a classical statue in the foreground, referencing the root of the story and a motif that runs through

Cocteau's work (the classical canon and classical art). The theme of 'the dream', so important to the Surrealists, is introduced as he says: 'This is all part of the same dream, the same nightmare.'

The sequence is presented as a camp melodrama with Jean Marais dressed and coiffured in the style of a matinee idol. He is acting melodramatically in an unremarkable domestic interior. When he hears of his wife's death, his dialogue is poetic and somewhat pretentious. This style of delivery suits the vain nature of the character as he says:

> 'I have spoken of her, I have dreamt
> of her, I've sung about her, I
> thought I knew her… but I didn't know
> her.'

As Orpheus is told that 'The Princess' is Death personified, he walks to the camera in a melodramatic shot that demonstrates Cocteau's roots as a writer of drama for the stage. The interior sequences are shot with fairly low-key lighting, harsh shadows on the wall betraying the artificial nature of the lighting design which could be read as anti-realist (it is actually more likely that the mid-shots are poorly executed with the lighting concentrated on the appropriate illumination for close-up shots of the characters). In these domestic interiors, the dialogue and themes appear to take precedence over the cinematic style (although in the special effects sequences, cinematic style takes centre stage). Buñuel also uses the language of melodrama, his black comedy appearing slightly more unsettling and less ironic than Cocteau's overplaying of the genre. Although the events of this sequence are more fantastic than those in *The Phantom of Liberty*, they make fewer demands on the viewer in terms of story logic; the events in the sequence make sense as the film has a supernatural element.

Orpheus is now told the 'secret of secrets' and the mirror theme appears as Heurtebise explains that mirrors are the doors through which death comes and goes. In a line that seems to acknowledge Oscar Wilde's *The Picture of Dorian Gray*, he says:

> 'Look in the mirror and you'll see
> death at work.'

In terms of his narrative function, Heurtebise now becomes the assistant who supplies the means and accompanies Orpheus on his quest to the underworld. In another example of Cocteau developing his own mythology, he tells Orpheus that a poet is 'more than a man' and can therefore enter the realm of death in order to retrieve Eurydice. This line of dialogue seems to identify the character (Orpheus) with the director (Cocteau); in contrast Buñuel's biographical references are developed with greater subtlety and seem less concerned with developing his own celebrity persona. In *The Phantom of Liberty*, Buñuel infuses the story with biographical details, attaching his own memories and anecdotes to a range of characters throughout the narrative. Cocteau seems more concerned with raising the figure of the poet (and thus himself) to mythical status.

Orpheus is now given some magic rubber gloves that will allow him to enter the mirror (Cocteau's trademark reverse filming is used as the gloves are donned in close-up). Cocteau now uses a range of simple but effective visual effects to introduce us to the fantasy element of the film as the characters pass from the bedroom into another world.

The first shot uses a handheld camera to show Orpheus's

point of view as he walks towards the mirror, hands outstretched. In this shot out of focus, gloved hands are held in the foreground as the camera approaches the 'reflection' of Orpheus in a mirror (as the camera is not seen in the mirror we are not seeing a 'real' reflection). We then cut to an overhead shot with the mirror at the bottom of the frame accompanied by the conventional fantasy sentiment 'you just have to believe'. We then cut to a close-up of a glove entering the mirror, achieved using reflective liquid and a camera rotated through 90 degrees. There is a cut back to the overhead shot as the two characters enter the mirror; the next shot is handheld and follows the characters as they disappear into their reflection (they are behind a glass door).

In an example of the type of symbolism used by Surrealist painters, the effects sequence is punctuated by a clock chiming and a postman delivering a letter (both symbols which feature in the Buñuel sequence discussed earlier). The final part of this sequence uses visual effects to show the two characters moving through a purgatory consisting of bombed-out buildings that act as a metaphor for the ruins of man's religion. In this sequence Heurtebise stands in the foreground with a back projection of Orpheus walking slowly, the camera tracking backwards in tandem. This, coupled with a wind machine and shadows cast across the foreground, gives the impression that Heurtebise is effortlessly floating through the scene while mortal Orpheus struggles. A glass vendor walks past Heurtebise and subsequently passes Orpheus, adding to the impression that they inhabit the same physical space. There is then a change of angle that allows the two men to be seen in the same shot, they join hands and arrive in the ruined land where the courtroom is located.

This sequence taken as a whole illustrates the themes and obsessions listed above, and demonstrates Cocteau's individual style and technique. It also illustrates areas of similarity and difference between the work of Cocteau and the other directors discussed in this book.

Critical Views

'*Orphée* updates a classic myth for modern audiences, referencing everything from French Resistance shortwave radios to Nazi bully boys and rock 'n' roll teenyboppers. Its real achievement, though, is in realising the power of cinema to bring fantasy to life. Using all kinds of inventive trick photography, Cocteau creates a dream-like universe in which the laws of physics no longer apply as people wander through mirrors and appear and disappear at will. Dominated by fetishistic imagery—Death is corseted into an hourglass black dress with elbow high rubber gloves; her motorcycle men stalk around in black leathers like rejects from the Village People—it's a breathlessly sexy film, charged with the lyrical eroticism of the fairy tale and fascinated by its own enchanting power. Once seen, it's never forgotten.' (Russell, 2004, BBC Films)

'The film is obsessed with death (and certainly Maria Casarès dominates it), but in Cocteau's version Orpheus and Eurydice are spared, saved by the self-sacrifice of Death and her suave assistant Heurtebise. Some might consider this sentimental. Younger audiences may think the special effects primitive, though because of their context and beautiful simplicity they are as superior to those in most recent fantasy pictures as Willis O'Brien's creations in *King Kong* tower over those of *Jurassic Park*.' (French, 2004, *The Observer*)

Filmography

Le Testament d'Orphée (The Testament of Orpheus) (1960)
8 X 8: A Chess Sonata in 8 Movements (1957)
La Villa Santo-Sospir (1952)
Coriolan (1950)
Orphée (Orpheus) (1950)
Les Parents terribles (The Storm Within) (1948)
L'Aigle à deux têtes (The Eagle Has Two Heads) (1948)
La Belle et la bête (Beauty and the Beast) (1946)
Le Sang d'un poète (The Blood of a Poet) (1930)

Jan Švankmajer and *Alice* (1988)

Jan Švankmajer (Born 1934)

Cast

Kristýna Kohoutová: Alice

Production Credits

Country: Czechoslovakia / Switzerland /UK /
                        West Germany
Language: English / Czech
Producer: Peter-Christian Fueter
Director: Jan Švankmajer
Writers: Jan Švankmajer from a story by
                        Lewis Carroll
Cinematography: Svatopluk Malý
Editing: Marie Zemanová

Jan Švankmajer is a Czech Surrealist who has created a distinct body of work with clear thematic and stylistic continuity. He made short films for more than 20 years before making his first feature length film in 1988. Švankmajer's films involve a combination of animation, puppetry and live action – a range of techniques with a distinctive unity of style that merge to create a disconcerting, personal, dream-like interpretation of the world.

Synopsis

An adaptation of the novel by Lewis Carroll in which a young girl named Alice travels to a strange subterranean dream world. She meets a stuffed white rabbit, a caterpillar made from a sock with false teeth, the Mad Hatter, the Mad March Hare and the Queen of Hearts. She is trapped in a number of strange interiors where scale and reason mean very little. The film combines animation and live action using a range of stop-motion and puppetry techniques.

Jan Švankmajer, like Luis Buñuel, is a film-maker who has attempted to use film as a medium for personal artistic expression and political/social comment. He has developed his work as a Surrealist under a different set of constraints. Although issues such as political censorship, funding difficulties and world events have conspired to restrict him, he has been able to develop and maintain a personal and highly influential style involving animation and live action. Again, like Buñuel, his work can also be split into three main phases:

1. Early films produced prior to the 'Prague Spring' of 1968.

2. Films made after 1968, mainly in Prague before the 1989 'Velvet Revolution'.

3. Films made after the 'Velvet Revolution' and the fall of Communism in Czechoslovakia.

Before describing his work in detail, it is worth offering a cultural context in order to help explain how Švankmajer developed his distinctive vision. In 1934 a Surrealist group was set up in Prague that built on the activities of the Parisian Surrealists led by André Breton. Breton, like Buñuel, had embraced Communism, mainly as a reaction against the rising tide of Fascism in Europe. He had visited Trotsky in Mexico and had attempted to create links between the Surrealist group and the French Communist Party. The Prague Surrealists had good relations with the Czechoslovakian communists but the Second World War and six years of Nazi rule curtailed any major development of the movement in Prague.

After the war, Czechoslovakia straddled the divide between the Soviet Union (Communist Russia) and the West (supported by America through the 'Marshall Plan'). Following poor harvests and the resulting food shortages, in 1948 the communists took charge and the Czech government forged strong links with Stalin's government in Russia. In the 'Prague Spring' of 1968 the Czech regime attempted to become more liberal and, as a result, Soviet-led forces invaded Czechoslovakia and installed a more oppressive regime. The country was effectively isolated from the west by the 'Iron Curtain' from 1948 to 1989. In 1993 the Czech Republic dissolved its federal union with Slovakia and the state of Czechoslovakia no longer existed.

This brief historical outline is relevant to Švankmajer's work as he began making films under the constraints of state communism, in a situation very different to that of film-makers working in Hollywood or western Europe. He would have had limited access to western cinema and art – his frame of reference would have been based on the folk and soviet culture that he experienced, supported by furtive underground glimpses of 'degenerate' western art and film.

The Prague Surrealist group that became established in 1934 continued to exist under communist rule. Švankmajer joined the group in 1969 and has continued to be a member and self-declared 'Militant Surrealist' until the present day. Many Czech film-makers were persecuted and exiled following the instalment of the post-1968 regime. Švankmajer managed to continue working, except for a brief government ban in the mid 1970s, throughout this period. He may have escaped persecution because he made short films that were seen to have a limited audience and therefore less of a potential threat to the state.

Švankmajer's background was in the arts and he continues to work in a range of media including painting and drawing. He studied at the Prague Academy of Fine Arts, working in the Marionette faculty where his long-standing interest in puppetry developed. Puppetry is the type of popular culture or folk art that inspired the founders of Surrealism, and is also the type of art that would be allowed to exist by the communist regime as being art of 'the people' (Surrealism, while tolerated, was seen more as an art of the degenerative bourgeois elite). Puppetry also has a strong element of the 'grotesque', an edge of mystery and magic combined with fear and fantasy (it is no coincidence that many horror films feature 'possessed' dolls and puppets).

Alice is the film that launched the third stage of Švankmajer's career, an adaptation of the *Alice* novels by Lewis Carroll. It builds on his earlier literary adaptations such as *The Fall of the House of Usher* (1981) and *The Pit, the Pendulum and Hope* (1983), both inspired by Edgar Allen Poe stories. He made a short adaptation of Lewis Carroll's poem *Jabberwocky* in

1971, and had long held an ambition to make a feature length version of *Alice's Adventures in Wonderland* and *Through the Looking Glass*. *Alice* was Švankmajer's ticket to creative freedom, its success coinciding with political liberation in eastern Europe. In some ways this parallels Buñuel's return to work in the European film industry after years of exile in Mexico. *Alice* was a co-production, funded by Switzerland, the UK and West Germany as well as Czechoslovakia. The film cemented his international reputation and allowed him to continue to make work in other countries, including two very short animations in 1989 for MTV in America (*Flora* and *Meat Love*).

The film has a linear narrative pattern where we follow one character through a range of absurd situations. The film sticks fairly closely to Carroll's story but infuses it with Švankmajer's distinctive vision, much of its power coming from his inventive and powerful animation technique. He attempts to bring inanimate objects to life in an almost magical ritual, believing that objects conceal the memory of events that they have witnessed. In *Alice*, he uses a 'cast' of three-dimensional artefacts from his own collection of antique and everyday objects alongside a single young actress to recreate the story of *Alice in Wonderland* from the perspective of a child's imagination.

Animation allows the film-maker to create effects that cannot happen in live action filming. Georges Méliès, Willis O'Brien and Ray Harryhausen understood this power and used it to create popular fantasy cinema such as the *King Kong* and *Sinbad* films. The growing dominance of CGI for special effects in films such as *The Matrix* is also testament to the importance of animation. Švankmajer uses this magical power as a means of subversion, to challenge the viewer's relationship with the animated objects that he depicts – to imbue the everyday with 'the uncanny'.

Švankmajer's early short films were relatively obscure and disjointed with jarring visuals and unconventional audio tracks; some feature bizarre combinations of live action, drawings and animated everyday objects; in others, the camera explores natural textures through edited sequences of camera movements. Characters in these films were often battling against inanimate objects and mysterious environments. *Alice* brings together themes, techniques and imagery from these earlier films, using them to realise a personal vision of the novel that relates closely to his own absurdist and black comic sensibility.

The entire film operates with the logic of a dream: in the opening sequence we are in a room but when the White Rabbit runs from the room we cut to a large ploughed field. The film moves seamlessly from one type of space to another, from one reality to the next – Alice doesn't appear to want to arrest this flow but follows it as we do in dreams. In the novel, Alice questions what is happening more often ('curiouser and curiouser') but in Švankmajer's *Alice*, the protagonist shows little emotion and the film-maker is not concerned with her emotions or psychological motivations. This is similar to Buñuel's approach in *The Phantom of Liberty* where characters are symbols rather than personalities. As Michael O'Pray says in his essay on Švankmajer's work:

'Surrealism, as his films admirably display, is not simply a matter of irrational fantasy: it also involves a particular relationship with the real and its properties.' (in Donald, 1989, p. 254)

Švankmajer continues to develop his ideas into the feature film format. In 1994, he made a version of Goethe's *Faust*, the story of a man who sells his soul to the devil. *Faust* uses a theatrical setting, mixing puppetry and live action to disconcerting effect; it acknowledges Švankmajer's own background and refers to the themes and content of other Surrealist films. *Conspirators of Pleasure* (1996) is a black comedy about obsession and desire that uses less animation and is a grotesque exploration of Surrealist themes such as sadism, rituals and magic. *Little Otik* (2000) is probably his most conventional film to date. It is a re-telling of a fairytale in which a childless couple fashion a baby from a tree stump; the wooden baby comes to life and proceeds to eat various visitors until the parents themselves are threatened. The story of *Little Otik* follows a conventional linear narrative structure and it has very little animation. It is still, however, a strange, disturbing and surreal film.

Švankmajer's Themes and Obsessions

There are a number of visual motifs and concepts that run through Švankmajer's work. Technical devices, particularly his highly individual animation techniques, camera movements and montage editing, support these themes:

Childhood and birth

Many of his films dwell on the irrational fears of childhood. *Alice* and *Little Otik* have children as the main protagonist. Often the world of the film is mediated through the imagination of children. Birth is shown in early animations such as *Dimensions of Dialogue* (1982) as well as in *Little Otik*. Toys are used extensively in his animations.

Cabinet of curiosities

The concept of alternative taxonomies or unusual collections of natural and bizarre objects was important to the Surrealists. Many of Švankmajer's films seem like the interior of an ancient museum with artefacts from natural history alongside food, toys and everyday objects. From the Renaissance onwards, before the advent of large public museums, it was popular for wealthy western individuals to collect together disparate specimens into 'Cabinets of Curiosity' or 'Wonder Rooms' (Wunderkammer). These private museums would combine ethnographic, geological and biological specimens with works of art, craft and historical relics. Often they would contain fictional objects (such as constructed creatures) and articles of faith (pieces of the 'true cross', etc.), alongside more conventional objects. In *Alice* Švankmajer creates rooms full of invented creatures that are constructed from animal remains combined with other objects. The film leads us through a number of these 'Wunderkammer' that make up the 'Wonderland' that Alice inhabits.

Puppetry

Puppets appear in many of Švankmajer's films combined with live action and animation, the result of his early training. Human characters often appear as puppets, subject to forces outside of their control. In *Alice*, the main character is turned into a doll and then back to a human. In *Faust* the main character appears to be possessed by spells and theatrics. In his early shorts such as *Dimensions of Dialogue*, Švankmajer uses a range of human characters combined with objects and models through stop-motion photography.

Folk tales, myths and legends

In a similar fashion to the horror genre, Švankmajer uses folk tales as the basis for many of his works. He often includes elements of gothic horror in his work such as monsters, madness, death, ruins, sadistic practices and decay. His early films such as *The Ossuary* (1970) and *Johann Sebastian Bach: Fantasy in G Minor* (1965) are documentaries featuring buildings and environments as metaphors of death and decay. In some of his early works, time lapse photography is used to show food and dead animals decaying. *Faust* and *Little Otik* feature monsters and devils – the sources of his narratives are often taken from or refer to folk tales (e.g. *Little Otik*) or gothic novels (e.g. *The Fall of the House of Usher*).

Altered states and the subconscious

The subconscious was a key concern of the Surrealists and many of Švankmajer's films concern madness and are structured as a dream or nightmare. He was used by the military to test LSD and this traumatic experience appears to have had an influence on the content of his work. During the Cold War, the Czechoslovak military were concerned that LSD might be used by the US Army as a chemical weapon. In the light of this concern, the military carried out research on conscripts and students to test the effect of LSD on their ability to perform as soldiers (see Alda, 2006). Švankmajer was 'tested' in this way in 1972. Although he denies that the experience had a major influence on his work, it is easy to see parallels between the nature of his work and the concept of altered states. He described his experience in an article for the *Guardian* newspaper:

*'They gave us the LSD intravenously. Then we lay there on
our beds, waiting for it to take effect. At first it was pleasant
enough, as the drug slowly began to take control. The first
phase was a kind of regression to infancy and a feeling of utter
helplessness. Then there were stroboscope-like effects: when
I raised my arm the movement would be broken up into a
series of static images, like a time-lapse shot, with a different
colour for each phase.'* (*The Guardian*, 19 October 2001)

He has said in his diary:

*'For me it was a terrifying experience from which it took years
to recover.'* (Švankmajer, 1999, *Kinoeye*)

Food and eating

Close-up shots of food and mouths eating feature heavily in
his work. Some of the early animations involve characters
eating each other. The connections between food, death and
decay are evident in a number of his films.

Analysis of a short sequence from Alice

The opening sequence of *Alice* can be used to illustrate
Švankmajer's technical style and thematic concerns. The first
five minutes of the film introduce us to Alice and the White
Rabbit, taking us from the everyday of the playroom to
a world of surreal fantasy.

There is a pre-credit sequence set in wet woodland. The
camera tracks along a river to rest on a young girl throwing
stones, sitting with an adult who is reading a book. Alice's
adult chaperone is anonymous, her head cropped by the
camera's framing, emphasising the child's perspective. The

adult smacks Alice for being nosey (Švankmajer's earlier adaptation of a Lewis Carroll poem, *Jabberwocky*, also has a child being punished in the opening sequence). The idea of 'repression' is a key element of Freudian theory; many surreal films include the elements of punishment and the repression of a child's imaginative play – surreal horrors such as the beast in *Little Otik* are often seen to spring from repressed fantasies.

In between the opening titles, Švankmajer uses his signature extreme close-up shot of a mouth. We can see this used in earlier shorts such as *Dimensions of Dialogue* and in later feature films such as *Little Otik*. The voice-over tells us 'this is a film for children...perhaps', intimating that Švankmajer's film (as with much animation) may appear to be aimed at children, but simultaneously deal with adult themes and create unsettling atmospheres. The hiding of radical messages or social critique within work for children or other conventional genres was a popular strategy that creative artists used in states under Soviet control to avoid censorship. Next, we have a typically surreal paradox when the voice-over says, 'now you must close your eyes, or you won't see anything'.

The post-credit sequence has Alice watching as the stuffed White Rabbit is brought to life. The soundtrack in this opening sequence is typical of Švankmajer's work in its use of isolated, exaggerated sound effects: a ticking clock, stones landing in a tea cup, a buzzing light bulb and the rustling of the stuffed rabbit. Buñuel used a similar palette of sound effects in the dream sequence from *The Phantom of Liberty* discussed earlier. Alice's playroom is explored by a roving camera, using a macro lens to explore details of an interior that reflects Švankmajer's previous work and some of the themes and obsessions mentioned above. The *mise-en-scène* is typical of the cluttered, worn, junk-shop interiors that feature in his early shorts: dark wooden furniture, institutional beds, desks and peeling paintwork in basement apartments. The camera passes a jar of buttons, framed collections of beetles and butterflies (also one of Buñuel's obsessions) and discarded apples cores (decaying fruit appear in many of Švankmajer's early shorts). Danger and death are hinted at by the trap laid for a mouse; Punch and Judy puppets refer to Švankmajer's early experience of puppetry at the marionette faculty of the Prague Academy of Fine Arts. The room can be seem an example of the 'wunderkammer' discussed earlier, it is also worth looking at the work of the Quay Brothers – particularly their tribute to Švankmajer, *The Cabinet of Jan Švankmajer* (1984) for an exploration and development of his motifs and *mise-en-scène*.

After this exploration of the room, the camera is used to show Alice's point of view as she watches the stuffed White Rabbit awake (the first animated sequence in the film). The rabbit's tongue is a similar animation to that used in *Dimensions of Dialogue* where clay figures have animated tongues constructed from cooked meat. The rabbit's clothes are kept in a drawer in the ground. Cabinets with drawers are a feature of Surrealist imagery (the paintings of Magritte and Dali, for example) and also appear in many of Švankmajer's films. The camera alternates between point of view shots, low angles and extreme close-ups for much of this sequence: this shows us Alice's point of view; the low angles make the viewer feel smaller and the close-ups create a feeling of claustrophobia.

As the rabbit leaves the room, crossing a fantastic threshold between the interior and a ploughed field, Švankmajer uses a handheld camera to show movement across the furrows. A desk sits in the field—the rabbit opens the drawer and disappears inside. Alice attempts to follow him and discovers that the drawer is full of geometric tools, devices from an old schoolroom used to measure and quantify an unquantifiable world. Alice climbs into the drawer and impossibly disappears as in a magician's trick. Švankmajer uses a combination of a simple split screen effect along with animated false legs as she finally vanishes into the drawer bringing to mind the work of Méliès, the early cinematic magician.

The sequence described demonstrates how Švankmajer uses *mise-en-scène* (and *mise-en-shot*) to illustrate his ideas and obsessions, creating a solipsistic mood of decay and entropy. The camera is used to animate inanimate objects; extreme close-ups and tracking shots explore the detail of an environment rich in symbolism. Live action is combined with animation and other conventional trick photography to create a disturbing vision of childhood.

Critical Views

'Nobody who has seen even one of Švankmajer's shorts is likely to doubt that the Czech Surrealist would make the definitive version of Lewis Carroll's *Alice's Adventures in Wonderland*. For no other film-maker—and that includes David Lynch—is so consistently inventive in his ability to marry pure, startling nonsense with rigorous logic, black wit with psychological insights.' (Andrew, in Pym (ed.) 2005, p.24)

'*Alice* is an 86-minute film, a 125,000-frame puzzle, and a meticulously constructed infantile dream. Jan Švankmajer has stated that he considers his childhood an equal partner in his life, a place easily and continually revisited: 'Childhood is my alter-ego.' As articulated in his art, Švankmajer's is not a nostalgic or distant childhood but an unsettling one saturated by a harassing malevolence, with puppet characters imbued with a disturbing ambiguity suspended between a static innocence and a moving, stalking dread.' (Bruyn, 2002, *Senses of Cinema*)

Filmography

Feature length films
Sílení (Lunacy) (2005)
Otesánek (Little Otik) (2000)
Spiklenci slasti (Conspirators of Pleasure) (1996)
Lekce Faust (Faust) (1994)
Neco z Alenky (Alice) (1988)

Short films produced after the 'Velvet Revolution' (the fall of Communism and the creation of the Czech Republic)
Jídlo (Food) (1992)
The Death of Stalinism in Bohemia (1990)
Animated Self-Portraits (1989)
Flora (1989)
Meat Love (1989)
Tma/Svetlo/Tma (Darkness/Light/Darkness) (1989)

Films made mainly in Prague before the 'Velvet Revolution'
Another Kind of Love (1988)
Muzné hry (Virile Games) (1988)
Do pivnice (Down to the Cellar) (1983)
Kyvadlo, jáma a nadeje (The Pit, the Pendulum and Hope) (1983)
Moznosti dialogu (Dimensions of Dialogue) (1982)
Zánik domu Usheru (The Fall of the House of Usher) (1981)
Otrantskýzámek (Castle of Otranto) (1977)
Leonarduv denik (Leonardo's Diary) (1972)
Zvahlav aneb Saticky Slameného Huberta (Jabberwocky) (1971)
Don Sanche (Don Juan) (1970)
Kostnice (The Ossuary) (1970)
Tichý týden v dome (A Quiet Week in the House) (1969)

Early films produced prior to the 'Prague Spring' of 1968

Byt (The Flat) (1968)

Picknick mit Weissmann (Picnic with Weissmann) (1968)

Zahrada (The Garden) (1968)

Historia Naturae, Suita (1967)

Et Cetera (1966)

Rakvickarna (Punch and Judy) (1966)

Hra s kameny (A Game with Stones) (1965)

Johann Sebastian Bach: Fantasy in G Minor (1965)

Poslední trik pana Schwarcewalldea a pana Edgara (The Last Trick) (1964)

David Lynch and *Lost Highway* (1997)

David Lynch (Born 1946)

Cast (selected)

Bill Pullman:	Fred Madison
Patricia Arquette:	Renee Madison/
	Alice Wakefield
Balthazar Getty:	Pete Dayton
Robert Blake:	Mystery Man
Natasha Gregson Wagner:	Sheila
Richard Pryor:	Arnie
Lucy Butler:	Candace Dayton
Michael Massee:	Andy
Jack Nance:	Phil
Jack Kehler:	Guard Johnny Mack
Henry Rollins:	Guard Henry
Giovanni Ribisi:	Steve 'V'
Scott Coffey	Teddy
Gary Busey:	Bill Dayton
Robert Loggia:	Mr Eddy/Dick Laurent

Production Credits

Country:	France / USA
Language:	English
Producer:	Deepak Nayar
Director:	David Lynch
Writers:	David Lynch and
	Barry Gifford
Cinematography:	Peter Deming
Editing:	Mary Sweeney
Music:	Angelo Badalamenti
	and David Lynch
Additional Music:	Marilyn Manson, Rammstein, David Bowie,
	Brian Eno, Nine Inch Nails

David Lynch was born in rural Montana and had a 'typical' all-American childhood. He attended art school, progressing from experimental shorts to feature films via the success of cult classic *Eraserhead* (1977). Much of his work depicts the stereotypes of the small-town America of his youth, juxtaposing them with the dark underbelly of American society, violent and degrading. Although Lynch's film and television work refers to many populist genres such as melodrama, film noir, soap opera, comedy and horror, he tends to work outside of mainstream Hollywood and has developed a loyal cult following – most markedly through his hit television series *Twin Peaks* (1990–92). He continues to produce work that challenges conventions; his most recent film, Inland *Empire* (2007), was shot on digital video and had only a limited theatrical release but prompted much critical debate.

Synopsis

Lost Highway is a horror/thriller/mystery film set in Los Angeles and based around the concept of 'identity crises'. A jazz musician (Fred Madison) is accused of killing his wife and found guilty, when in jail he changes into another character (Pete Dayton) who appears to have suffered a memory loss. Pete is set free and goes back to his family and his work at a garage. Here he meets Alice Wakefield, who is physically identical to Madison's murdered wife. Alice is the girlfriend of a gangster (Mr Eddy). Pete is drawn into a web of deceit resulting in their involvement with drugs, pornography and murder. The film has scenes of strong sex and violence.

David Lynch has been described as the foremost Surrealist in the history of Hollywood. Although we are focusing on world cinema in this book, it is worth considering Lynch in order to see how the high production values and large budgets of Hollywood studio productions can expand the language and techniques of Surrealism into mainstream popular culture.

Lynch's films and television work refer to many populist genres such as melodrama, film noir, soap opera, comedy and horror. His films appear to reflect the small town America of Frank Capra's films: the term 'Capraesque' was coined to describe the atmosphere of the films that Capra made with James Stewart in the 1940s where an ordinary individual in a small town could change the world through small acts of everyday courage (*It's a Wonderful Life*, 1946, being the best known example). David Lynch was described by his early mentor, Mel Brooks, as 'Jimmy Stewart from Mars' (Rodley, 1996, p. 6), illustrating how Capra's wholesome sensibility is tempered in Lynch's work by dark undercurrents of criminality, depravity and sadistic sexuality. Much of the power of Surrealist film comes from the depiction of ordinary, everyday reality reconstructed in such a way as to tap into the subconscious.

Although often aligned with Surrealism, Lynch claims to have had little knowledge of Buñuel or other Surrealists when making his early work (latterly he has claimed Breton as an influence). He does, however, claim that his writing process involves the use of the subconscious: dreams and daydreams are used to inform and create the narrative. This process is a direct parallel to the technique that Buñuel and Dali used for *Un chien andalou*. Like the early Surrealists, Lynch is known to include chance encounters and mistakes during filming in the final product. These techniques leave his films open to psychoanalytical study, although Lynch tends to shy away from this approach, preferring mystical explications and puzzles as keys to his movies: as an example, consider the 'clues' that accompanied the DVD release of *Mulholland Dr.* (2001). These ten 'clues' provided by Lynch himself are similar to the type of cod psychoanalysis that we see in Hitchcock's *Spellbound* (1945) – but are intended more as Lynch's own personal, consciously intended, allegorical language.

Lynch's 10 'clues' to *Mulholland Dr.*

1. Pay particular attention to the beginning of the film: at least two clues are revealed before the credits.

2. Notice appearances of the red lampshade.

3. Can you hear the title of the film that Adam Kesher is auditioning actresses for? Is it mentioned again?

4. An accident is a terrible event... notice the location of the accident.

5. Who gives a key, and why?

6. Notice the robe, the ashtray, the coffee cup.

7. What is felt, realised and gathered at the club Silencio?

8. Did talent alone help Camilla?

9. Note the occurrences surrounding the man behind Winkies.

10. Where is Aunt Ruth?

Lost Highway (1997) was Lynch's first feature film for five years, following the poor reception for *Twin Peaks: Fire Walk with Me* in 1992. The opening page of the script describes *Lost Highway* as *'A 21st century Noir Horror film. A graphic investigation into parallel identity crises. A world where time is dangerously out of control.'* (www.lynchnet.com/lh)

Although Lynch says this description of the film is 'sort of baloney' (Rodley, 1996, p. 6), the film *is* a mystery, not only to the viewer but also to the actors (and possibly even to Lynch himself). His films have always confounded easy classification, using elements from a range of genres and refusing to conform to the standard expectations of Hollywood. To understand *Lost Highway*, it is important to have an idea of how Lynch's previous work was conceived and received.

Lynch was born in rural Missoula, Montana. Lynch has discussed how he felt at home in small town America, finding the big cities noisy and frightening. This type of binary opposition between town and country, good and evil is a feature of his work. He went to art school where he made short films. Lynch's first films were a combination of live action and animation; similar in some ways to the themes and mood of Švankmajer's early work. *The Alphabet* (1968) is a short film that, like Buñuel's *Un chien andalou*, is based on a dream and, like the films discussed previously, uses strange sound effects and wild sounds combined to heighten the chimerical atmosphere.

Following the success of his early short films, Lynch made the cult classic *Eraserhead* (completed in 1977 after five years of work with friends and relatives, shooting in abandoned buildings and studio back-lots).

Eraserhead was shot in black and white using bleak, sinister *mise-en-scène* and low-key lighting. Like *Lost Highway*, the film combines film noir, horror and science fiction. It follows the relationship between Henry Spencer and his girlfriend, Mary X. They live in what appears to be an abandoned, post-apocalyptic industrial town explored using the style of low-budget horror with an avant-garde experimental structure and character development that follows the dream-like logic of the early Surrealists. After its initial theatrical release, the film's popularity grew slowly to be an underground success, popular with students and late-night horror fans. A cult grew up around the film, with fans endlessly discussing the meaning of its strange scenes and peculiar characters. The film established Lynch as a new American director with a distinctive vision and style.

After the underground success of *Eraserhead*, Lynch was offered the opportunity to work on a more conventional film with a large budget, an established cast and a professional crew. This film was *The Elephant Man* (1980). It was nominated for eight Oscars and although the method of production and narrative are distinctly different from *Eraserhead*, the film has a similar black and white aesthetic with gothic fantasy sequences such as the nightmare vision of Merrick's conception and his final dream. The carnival, freak shows and grotesquery are also themes and passions of the early Surrealists, Buñuel and Švankmajer.

On the back of *The Elephant Man's* critical success, Lynch worked with an even larger budget of $45 million (still a significant budget over twenty years later) on an adaptation of Frank Herbert's popular science fiction novel *Dune* (1984). This film has recently been re-evaluated after a hostile reception on release. Lynch experienced a range of technical and personal problems that often accompany Hollywood blockbusters, particularly when they involve complex sets, special effects and multiple locations. In addition, *Dune* is the only one of his films on which he did not have 'final cut' (i.e. the contractual promise that the producer can not alter the director's final print). The re-issued 'special edition' of *Dune* has offered us the opportunity to see beyond the sprawling narrative, the broadly drawn characters and the poor critical reputation, to see themes and moods that have appeared throughout Lynch's body of work. A number of the cast members continued to work with Lynch post-*Dune*. If you are aware of Lynch's more successful work such as the television series *Twin Peaks* (1990–1) and *Blue Velvet* (1986), it is interesting to see these actors transposed from small town America into a future that combines the Victorian interiors of *The Elephant Man* with the spaceships, rubber suits and other conventions of the science fiction genre. (This type of analysis of a body of work backwards and forwards in time is not only a great example of *auteur* study but also an interesting way to look at how the advent of the DVD has allowed revision and re-assessment of film texts.)

After the poor critical and box office reception of *Dune*, Lynch bounced back with what is considered by many to be his signature work, *Blue Velvet*. It is set in the small town America of his childhood and features dark subversive themes such as sadomasochism, drugs, prostitution and criminality. The film style is a pastiche of 1950s American culture, television soap opera and the horror/thriller genre. In many ways, the scenes of everyday life such as the slow motion shots of tulips, picket fences and fire engines in the film's opening sequence are more unreal and disturbing than the scenes of sexual deviance and suspense that follow. It is worth analysing the opening sequence of the film in depth to see how the camera moves with great economy from the comfortable surface of society to its dark underbelly represented by the severed ear buried in the neatly manicured lawn. The success of *Blue Velvet* led directly to the mainstream success of Lynch's cult TV show, *Twin Peaks* (via the Palme d'Or winning *Wild at Heart*, 1990). The combination of genres from which *Twin Peaks* was constructed can be seen as the first postmodern ironic drama series and its influence is felt in series such as *Six Feet Under* (2001–5) and *Desperate Housewives* (2004–). *Twin Peaks* ran for two series and spawned a feature film prequel, *Twin Peaks: Fire Walk with Me*.

Following the experience of working with a large budget and a major studio on *Dune* and despite the success of *Twin Peaks*, Lynch has concentrated on relatively smaller budgets and more personal films such as *Lost Highway*, although the film can hardly be considered 'independent' or low budget, featuring known stars and high production values. What the film does demonstrate is a personal vision and a willingness to work outside of the conventional expectations of Hollywood narrative and genre films. Lynch has continued further down this road and his most recent film at the time of writing, *Inland Empire* (2006), is arguably his most formally experimental since his debut.

There is a dark atmosphere to *Lost Highway*; created by Lynch carefully investing each shot with visual and emotional depth. The dialogue is half-whispered as if characters are uncertain of themselves or their place in the narrative. Comments from the cast and crew illustrate how this mood of solipsistic uncertainty was reached: Lynch explains that the two characters played by Patricia Arquette are the same person whereas she believes that she plays 'two different interpretations of the same woman' (Rodley, 1996, p. 10). Natasha Wagner (who plays Sheila in the film) says that the interpretation of the script is 'up to everyone's imagination: the audiences and the actors playing the roles' (Rodley, 1996,

p. 8). This lack of compulsion in the film's narrative allows for multiple readings – an example of what Roland Barthes calls 'the terror of uncertain signs' (Barthes, 1977, p. 39). There is no definitive answer to the meaning of the film. This uncertainty is the key surreal element of the film.

The condition that Fred Madison (Bill Pullman) suffers from has been described by Lynch as a 'psychogenic fugue' (www.lynchnet.com/lh); this is a condition where someone takes on a different personality and lives two parallel lives. With this in mind, it is interesting to compare *Lost Highway* to Buñuel's *Cet obscur objet du désir*. In Buñuel's film we have one character played by two actresses; in Lynch's, two characters played by one actress. Both films play with notions of identity and sexual obsession.

Lost Highway references Lynch's other films, using actors from *Twin Peaks* and *Eraserhead* and long-time musical collaborator, Angelo Badalamenti (the score was recorded in Prague with the same orchestra that was used for *Blue Velvet*). The orchestral score is complemented by the use of Lynch's trademark low frequency sounds (particularly in Fred and Renee's house). *Blue Velvet* is also referred to in the scene where Pete returns home and is seen sitting on his sun lounger in the garden.

Indeed *Lost Highway* can be seen as an up-dated *Blue Velvet*, leaving behind the nostalgia for the 1950s America of Lynch's youth and reflecting on his position as an established Hollywood film-maker struggling to forge an identity amongst the apocalyptic fears of the encroaching new millennium.

Lynch's Themes and Obsessions

Lynch has managed to develop and maintain his persona as a cult director through his website www.davidlynch.com and through encouraging his fan base to identify themes and discuss the enigmatic riddles that inhabit his films (he even sells his own brand of organic coffee on-line). There are a number of extensive Lynch fan-sites and an international community of *Twin Peaks* fans. His forays into the horror, fantasy and science fiction genres would help to support this cult fan base. The following are just a few of the themes and obsessions that run through his work:

Dreams

This archetypal Surrealist theme appears in many of his films. Dreams are used to structure narratives such as Agent Cooper's dreams in *Twin Peaks*. The distinction between dream and reality is often blurred and characters will not question the power or significance of dreams that are often taken as an extension of reality.

Low frequency, ambient noise

Subtle use of disconcerting audio tones turns up in many of his films, alongside the use of popular music. We often hear machine noises and strange ambient backgrounds: this has featured in his work since *Eraserhead*.

Small town America

Everyday life away from the urban centres and a harking back to an idealised 1950s America are often the focus of his movies.

The forest

Mystical happenings, threats and strange characters are often connected with woodland or wilderness areas. Log cabins, shacks and old railway carriages are the sites of important, sinister events in the narrative (see, for example, *Lost Highway* and *Twin Peaks*).

Red curtains

Specific elements of *mise-en-scène* in Lynch films have been identified as frequently re-occuring. Examples are red curtains, piles of earth, decay, low-key lighting, strobe lights and smoke.

Casting

Among his frequently used actors are Kyle MacLachlan, Laura Dern, Jack Nance, Everett McGill, Isabella Rossellini, Dean Stockwell, Brad Dourif, Sherilyn Fenn and Sheryl Lee.

Analysis of a short sequence from *Lost Highway*

Below is an analysis of a short sequence from *Lost Highway* that illustrates some of Lynch's trademarks and the relationship of his work to Surrealism and fantasy cinema. The sequence is approximately 13 minutes long, following Fred and Renee from the party at Andy's house, back to their own apartment where Renee is murdered. The sequence is from the first half of the film; it starts at approximately 27 minutes and ends at 40 minutes.

The sequence opens at Andy's upmarket Hollywood party;

there is a swimming pool and 'beautiful people' predominate. Surrealists such as Buñuel often used cinema to dissect and analyse the lives of the rich 'bourgeoisie'. Lynch also uses cinema to investigate society, from a personal/psychological perspective rather than the more overtly political critique of the early Surrealists. The autobiographical nature of Lynch's work can be seen in the move from narratives about small town America (*Blue Velvet*, *Twin Peaks*) to stories based in the more alienated world of Hollywood (*Lost Highway*, *Mulholland Dr.*).

Fred orders a drink at the bar, 'cheesy' 90s dance music plays in the background. The scene is shot in a conventional style using a range of shot sizes and shot/reverse shot as Fred scans the room to see the a strange white-faced man in the crowd. The 'Mystery Man' catches Fred's eye and walks purposefully towards him. As he moves into close-up, the diegetic disco music reverberates and fades out to be replaced by the type of accentuated ambient sound used in Lynch's other films (and also in the previously discussed extracts of Buñuel and Švankmajer's work). This change in the audio track is the main indicator that something supernatural or disturbing is happening. The clown-like appearance of the Mystery Man (played by Robert Blake) adds to the effect; similar spectres have featured in other of Lynch's work including 'Killer Bob' and 'The Man From Another Place' in *Twin Peaks*. The previous small-talk is replaced by an ominous, sinister and assertive closed question from the Mystery Man in extreme close-up:

> 'We've met before,
> haven't we?'

Fred is immediately confused by the question and by the aura of this man, who goes on to say:

> `'We met at your house…`
> `as a matter of fact, I'm`
> `there right now.'`

It is at this point that we clearly begin to enter the world of fantasy, the point that Todorov describes as 'that hesitation experienced by a person who knows only the laws of nature, confronting an apparently supernatural event' (Gelder, 2000, p. 15). From this point on in the film, we are no longer sure exactly how to 'read' the narrative; elements such as character, realism, internal and external experience start to become uncertain. It is this element of dream-like fantasy and the lack of clear explication at the end of the film that make *Lost Highway* a Surrealist work. We see Fred's uncertainty and begin to empathise with him; we share his emotions as we try to work out how the Mystery Man can answer the telephone at Fred's house – is it just a clever party trick or is he really in two places at once? As the character walks away from Fred, the dance music fades in again and we are back in the 'reality' of the party. The music and close-up photography has been effectively used in this encounter to create an intense psychological space that we share with the two characters. Fred is now paranoid and disorientated, and suggestions of intimacy between Renee and Andy are subtly suggested through careful direction of the actors' gaze and posture. Obsessive sexual jealousy is a key theme of this film and one that runs through the history of Surrealist cinema from *Un chien andalou*, through *That Obscure Object of Desire* and *Blue Velvet* to contemporary films such as *Being John Malkovich* (1999).

Fred and Renee leave the party and drive home. As they arrive, the interior of their home is temporarily lit – is there someone inside (cue mysterious music) or is it just the car's headlights? The expensive, minimalist home is a symbol of Fred (and possibly Lynch's) alienation, a contrast to the more homely interiors of *Twin Peaks* and *Blue Velvet*. There is ominous music as Fred enters the house alone and explores its red-curtained interior; low-key lighting and expressionistic camerawork are used to illustrate Fred's disturbed and paranoid mental state. We are made to jump as the telephone rings and a whip pan reveals Fred looking ill and disturbed. Fred paces around, casting large shadows, as Renee gets ready for bed. Throughout this section of the sequence, very little colour is used except for the red headboard of the bed and Lynch's trademark red curtains. A deep, resonant bass sound is used as Fred vanishes into the dark, labyrinthine corridors of his modernist house. Renee calls his name and Fred reappears from the shadows as the soundtrack rumbles, walking directly towards the camera to obscure the lens. The dialogue has become minimal, the two characters are seen to be isolated and alienated – this part of the sequence is closest to Lynch's earlier work such as *Eraserhead*.

We next see Fred in long shot, entering the living room (which is now more brightly lit). He puts a videotape into the player and we see the content of the tape in grainy black and white: A wide angle tracking shot takes us into Fred's bedroom where Renee is lying dead on the floor. The scene flashes an almost subliminal colour shot (freezing the DVD reveals a dismembered body, blood covering the bed, Fred standing over the body). The soundtrack becomes discordant as Fred shouts 'Renee!!'. Lightning flashes across his face and we cut to the next scene as a police officer punches Fred and the interrogation begins.

This sequence alone features a number of Lynch's trademark motifs (low frequency noises, red curtains and dream-like elements). In its use of conventional cinematic genres and techniques to create discomfort and uncertainty in the viewer (through mystery and the exploration of psychological states) it parallels the work of Buñuel and other cinematic Surrealists.

Critical Views

David Lynch has said of his film work: 'mystery is good, confusion is bad'. He tries to create psychological mysteries that force us to question the subjective nature of reality: 'we're not experiencing the ultimate reality: the "real" is hiding all through life, but we don't see it.' (Rodley, (ed.), 2005, p.227)

Below are some other views on this film:

'There's no need to even try to make sense of the plot: Lynch, who co-wrote the script with *Wild at Heart* author Barry Gifford, is merely playing around with the idea of twisted, intertwined fates and the notion of the eternal return. This movie's big "meanings" are actually the most insignificant things about it. Aspiring to be the most artful and profound Lynch film yet, *Lost Highway* is really his most facile.' (Zacharek, 1997, *Salon Magazine*)

'David Lynch's *Lost Highway* is like kissing a mirror: You like what you see, but it's not much fun, and kind of cold. It's a shaggy ghost story, an exercise in style, a film made with a certain breezy contempt for audiences. I've seen it twice, hoping to make sense of it. There is no sense to be made of it. To try is to miss the point. What you see is all you get.' (Ebert, 1997, *Chicago Sun-Times*)

Filmography

Feature films
Inland Empire (2006)
Mulholland Dr. (2001)
The Straight Story (1999)
Lost Highway (1997)
Twin Peaks: Fire Walk with Me (1992)
Wild at Heart (1990)
Blue Velvet (1986)
Dune (1984)
The Elephant Man (1980)
Eraserhead (1977)

Other selected film, TV and video work
Rammstein: Lichtspielhaus (2003, music video)
Rabbits (2002)
The Short Films of David Lynch (2002 a DVD compilation of early shorts)
Darkened Room (2002)
Twin Peaks (1990) (TV Series episodes - pilot, 1.2, 2.1, 2.2, 2.7, 2.22)

Early short films
The Amputee (1974)
The Grandmother (1970)
The Alphabet (1968)
Six Figures Getting Sick (1966)

Jeunet and Caro and *La Cité des enfants perdus /*
The City of Lost Children (1995)

Jean-Pierre Jeunet (Born 1953) and Marc Caro (Born 1956)

Cast

Ron Perlman:	One
Daniel Emilfork:	Krank
Judith Vittet:	Miette
Dominique Pinon:	The Clones
Jean-Claude Dreyfus:	Marcello
Geneviève Brunet:	The Octopus
Odile Mallet:	The Octopus
Mireille Mossé:	Miss Bismuth
Serge Merlin:	Gabriel Marie (Cyclops Leader)
Rufus:	Peeler
Ticky Holgado:	Ex-acrobat
Joseph Lucien:	Denree
Marc Caro:	Brother
	Ange-Joseph
Jean-Louis Trintignant:	Uncle Irvin (voice)

Production Credits

Country:	France/Germany/Spain
Language:	French
Producer:	Claudie Ossard
Director:	Jean-Pierre Jeunet and Marc Caro
Writers:	Jean-Pierre Jeunet, Marc Caro and Gilles Adrien
Cinematography:	Darius Khondji
Editing:	Hervé Schneid
Music:	Angelo Badalamenti

Jeunet and Caro are French film-makers who worked together as co-directors on two successful feature films; *Delicatessen* (1991) and *The City of Lost Children* (1995). They started working together in the 1970s and, since the success of their collaborative work, have taken different routes: Jeunet has continued to direct highly successful films, including time spent in Hollywood as director of *Alien Resurrection* (1997) and the internationally popular French film *Amélie* (2001). Caro moved into smaller-scale multimedia work and has just completed shooting a science fiction feature in France, *Dante 01* (2007).

Synopsis

The evil scientist Dr Krank lives on an isolated rig surrounded by mines, just off the coast of a busy, grimy port city. Sharing his floating laboratory are six identical cloned 'brothers', the diminutive Miss Bismuth and Uncle Irvin (a disembodied brain floating in a Victorian fish tank with a camera lens for an eye). Krank is dying of old age and is unable to dream. He enlists a quasi-religious group of 'cyclops' to help him abduct children from the city in order to steal their dreams.

The port is inhabited by, among others, a circus strongman named One and his foundling brother, Denree. When Denree is abducted by the Cyclops, One enlists the help of a streetwise orphan named Miette who is the leader of a gang living under the control of the Siamese twins known as The Octopus.

One and Miette work together to free Denree and the other children from the clutches of Krank and the Cyclops. They have to beat Krank and his 'family' by entering the dream he is sharing with Denree.

For the final fantasy *auteur*, we will consider the work of a creative duo who have worked together on feature films for only a relatively short period, but creating a number of distinctive films. There are a few examples of effective directing partnerships in film history such as the Coen brothers or Michael Powell and Emeric Pressburger ('The Archers') but directing is generally a solo occupation for both practical and industrial reasons.

Jeunet and Caro are aware of the importance of the co-operative nature of film production and, like most successful directors, gathered together a group of (mostly French) creative individuals who give their joint film work a distinctive style and atmosphere. They split the work evenly with Caro concentrating on the *mise-en-scène* and Jeunet working closely with the actors.

Jean-Pierre Jeunet began his career directing short videos and television commercials. Marc Caro started out as an artist and comic book creator. They met in the late 1970s and made three short movies together, winning awards and briefly going their separate ways to work on individual projects before working together on their first feature film, *Delicatessen*, in 1991. *Delicatessen* was an international success, winning awards at home and abroad. The film is a science fiction fantasy set in an apocalyptic future where nothing much grows and food is scarce. Dominique Pinon, the unusual actor who is a regular member of their creative team, plays a circus clown who comes to live and work in a butcher's run-down apartment block. The apartments are inhabited by a range of strange and grotesque characters including the landlord who kills and mutilates tenants in order to sell the flesh to the other residents. The film also involves a group of subterranean vegetarian freedom fighters and an unusual love story between the butcher's daughter and Pinon's character (Louison).

The international success of *Delicatessen* allowed Jeunet and Caro to develop and fund a project that they had started to write ten years earlier, *La Cité des enfants perdus (The City of Lost Children)*. This is a complex fantasy narrative with stunning visual effects and a highly stylised *mise-en-scène* that builds on the look and style of *Delicatessen*. The directors worked closely with French digital effects companies to create some innovative sequences such as a teardrop that sets in action a fantastic sequence of events; a flea's-eye view of the world; and the artificial vision of the auto-blinded Cyclops characters, who blind themselves in order to join a religious cult. The action takes place in a dark, futuristic fantasy port where a strongman called One develops a relationship with a young girl in order to find his abducted baby brother. His brother has been taken by the evil Dr Krank who lives on an offshore rig where he attempts to steal the dreams of children. *La Cité des enfants perdus* was produced with mainly French talent and, although not quite as critically successful as *Delicatessen* internationally, it led to offers of work from Hollywood for Jeunet. He worked on the 1997 *Alien Resurrection* exporting some of his team to Hollywood (including, initially, Caro who worked as design supervisor).

Caro went his own way to develop his interest in multimedia projects (*La Cité des enfants perdus* was also produced as a Playstation game) as well as acting in and directing smaller projects. On his return to France, Jeunet made the fabulously successful *Le Fabuleux destin d'Amélie Poulain (Amélie)* (2001). In this work, he used the style of his previous films but softened the atmosphere to create a nostalgic vision of the Montmartre area of Paris. The film brought actress Audrey Tatou to the world's attention and it contains elements of biography, making it Jeunet's most personal and individual film to date. His latest release, *Un long dimanche de fiançailles (A Very Long Engagement*, 2005) had the third largest budget ever for a French film (Euro 46 Million) and again features Tatou, developing the romantic content that was the focus of *Amélie* whilst also showing the horror of trench warfare in the First World War.

The creative partnership of Jeunet and Caro may reform one day but their feature filmography currently consists of two creatively distinctive films that depict a nightmare fantasy view of the future tempered with black comedy and sentimental nostalgia.

Historical and Social Context

In considering the context of *La Cité des enfants perdus*, it is worth (very) briefly outlining the development of French national cinema*. As early as 1918, after the First World War had devastated much of the European film industry, French cinemas were swamped with American films. In response, the European studio bosses forged agreements in the early 1920s,

(* For an extended introduction to these issues, see Martine Danan's essay in Fowler, 2002, pp. 232-43.)

attempting to produce high profile, spectacular European films that could compete with the Hollywood imports and appeal to world audiences.

The development of film sound in the late 1920s led to an awareness at government level of the importance of French national cinema in developing and maintaining national identity (particularly the importance of protecting the French language). In 1946 the *Centre National de la Cinématographie* (CNC) was established to protect French cinema as a national institution. The CNC provided financial incentives for the industry, established guidelines and protected production by creating a fund to support French film-making. The fund received revenue via a tax on all ticket sales and (from 1985) television earnings. The fund has been used ever since to support all French production with extra resources given to 'quality' products (often perceived as lower budget films by new directors with 'artistic integrity').This level of government support enabled the French New Wave directors to establish themselves in the 1950s and 1960s and, via their critical writings, to propagate the belief in film as an art form and the director as *auteur*.

Towards the end of the 1980s, with the growth of multinational media conglomerates, the CNC began to support larger European co-productions, even allowing English language films to be supported such as *Valmont* (1989) and *1492: Conquest of Paradise* (1992) – films that promoted French heritage in a similar way to the Merchant Ivory vision of Britain. *La Cité des enfants perdus* was funded by (among others) CNC, Eurimages (an organisation initiated by the French government to support European co-productions) and Canal Plus (the French 'semi-public' television channel). This type of mixed funding between commercial, government and European institutions is seen as essential if big budget

115

French films aimed at a large international audience are to be produced. *La Cité des enfants perdus* can thus be seen to be a product of state subsidy as well as pointing the way towards a new 'postnational' French cinema of nostalgia. In this regard Jeunet's latest film (*Un long dimanche de fiançaille*) has become involved in an argument as to its nationality due to the level of funding received from America – despite being a film in French about a French subject with a French cast and crew.

Narrative Structure, Characters and Themes

La Cité des enfants perdus has a fairly conventional circular narrative structure with a similar dream forming both the opening and penultimate sequences. The narrative progresses in a linear fashion with only two flashback sequences. Conventional film narratives tend to follow the pattern outlined by Tzvetan Todorov (Gelder, 2000, p. 19):

1. The film will open with a state of equilibrium or balance.

2. Something will disrupt this equilibrium (a catalytic event).

3. There will be a quest to restore equilibrium.

4. The film will end with a new equilibrium (usually a happy ending).

In *La Cité des enfants perdus*, the events follow straightforward cause–effect logic. The equilibrium is shown initially by the first sequence in the City, where One and Denree are working together. This is immediately disrupted by the abduction of Denree; One is now on a quest to find his lost 'brother'. The antagonist is introduced as Krank, who is in alliance with the Cylops. One has to overcome this axis of power in order to save his brother and establish a new equilibrium. As One progresses on his quest, he meets a number of helpers and encounters a range of obstacles. His first helper is Miette, who joins him on the quest. They find a route to the rig via other helpers (Irvin, who sends the nightmare message, and the tattooist, who reveals the map on his bald head). Just as they are about to leave, armed with this information, another obstacle appears in the form of the Octopus. Happily saved by chance and another helper, Marcello, they are able to continue on their quest that leads to the destruction of Krank.

The back story of the film or 'exposition' is related by Uncle Irvin in the form of a fairytale type narrative. The Diver's exposition is in the form of a sudden recovery of memory or 'flashback' triggered by the nightmare sent from Irvin. In some ways the resolution of the narrative is less than satisfying as there is no real transformation of One's character. The new equilibrium suggests that One, Miette and Denree form a new family group and, on a separate boat, Irvin leads the clones to new life.

In Krank's desire to become human, the film considers what it means to be human and makes us explore the nature of 'monstrosity'. The film deals with naive sexuality and has been accused of suggesting a sexual relationship between One and the nine-year-old Miette. In response to this, Jeunet states that the sexual connotations are:

'unconscious on the part of the little girl...and with us, too: it was while editing that we realized it'. (see www.sonyclassics. com/city/misc/interview.html)

Much of the pleasure of *La Cité des enfants perdus* comes from the fantasy scenario and the stunning visuals. Marc Caro was involved closely with the production design, developing the *mise-en-scène* to suggest a complete fantasy universe. Caro intended to create a 'retro future...very Jules Verne, with The

Nautilus, also Frankenstein's laboratory, with the bolts etc.' (see www.sonyclassics.com/city/misc/interview.html). The characters in this universe are clad in costumes created by the outré fashion designer Jean-Paul Gaultier.

One of the most important contributors to the visual style of the film is the cinematographer, Darius Khondji. He worked on *Delicatessen* and has also worked on a number of other visually powerful films. He was cinematographer on David Fincher's *Se7en* (1995) and *Panic Room* (2002). He has also worked on films as diverse as Jeunet's *Alien Resurrection*, Woody Allen's *Anything Else* (2003), *Wimbledon* (2004), and Sydney Pollack's stylish thriller, *The Interpreter* (2005). Khondji uses a film processing technique known the 'silver retention process' that allows very dark blacks and de-saturates the image to create washed out colours and high contrast. Another important element of *La Cité des enfants perdus* is the musical score, composed by Angelo Badalamenti, who has worked with David Lynch on films such as *Blue Velvet*, *Twin Peaks*, *Lost Highway* and *Wild at Heart*.

La Cité des enfants perdus was relatively successful but not as popular with critics as *Delicatessen* or as successful with audiences as Jeunet's next French film, *Amélie*.

Jeunet and Caro's Themes and Obsessions

Dreams

Jeunet and Caro's films have a dream-like quality, even using dream sequences as part of the narrative development. Jeunet sees dreams as essential to the art of the film-maker: 'If one cannot dream and imagine things, and if one is sentenced to the everyday, to reality, it's awful' (see www.sonyclassics.com/city/misc/interview.html).

Chance encounters

The teardrop scene from *La Cité des enfants perdus* triggers a chain of chance events that saves the lives of the two protagonists. Chance and fate structure the narrative of Jeunet's *Amélie*.

Carnivals and circus

The carnival and the fairground attracted the first Surrealists and the influence of this has been briefly discussed earlier. Louison from *Delicatessen* is a retired clown, One from *La Cité des enfants perdus* is a circus strongman; we also see flea trainers, Siamese twins and ghost trains in their films.

Nostalgia

The ornate, Jules Verne-style *mise-en-scène*, low-key lighting and de-saturated colour all foster a nostalgia for a bygone France. Yet this nostalgia always contains an element of threat and is never entirely comforting.

Orphans

Main characters in Jeunet and Caro's films are often orphans. We see children living on the streets or in orphanages. Some children are foundlings, others have lost one or both parents. Childhood features in their films with naive or childlike adults alongside child characters (a theme present even in the Hollywood blockbuster, *Alien Resurrection*).

The body

As with Buñuel, physical disabilities feature in their films; facial disfigurement, accidents of birth and extremes of size may be central to the narrative or appear as secondary elements.

Distortion

Matching the distorted characters and personalities, Jeunet and Caro often make use of very wide angled and distorting lenses to emphasise faces and architecture. The 'silver retention process' is used to create a de-saturated, almost monochrome, look.

Casting

Jeunet and Caro have a number of actors who they use regularly – Caro himself also acts in their films.

Analysis of a short sequence from *La Cité des enfants perdus*

The scene analysed below is from approximately 1 hour 13 minutes into the film. It includes the attempted assassination of One and Miette by 'The Octopus'–the DVD chapter is titled 'It all started with a tear'.

The sequence opens in a deserted dockland at night. The *mise-en-scène* of this sequence is dominated by the use of water and a mysterious yellow mist that envelops the port. Miette and One are both wearing striped Bretonic knitwear. Costume designer, Jean-Paul Gaultier, is in many ways representative of a contemporary French Surrealist style. He is known in the UK as co-presenter of the late-night TV show *Eurotrash*, and is an icon of Parisian avant-garde culture.

After establishing the location, the camera shifts to an extreme macro close-up of an animated flea next to a cigar butt that fills the screen. As we have seen, insects feature heavily in Surrealist work as symbolic and other worldly creatures (it is not always easy to define the precise symbolism of surrealism in film but it appears and relates to dream imagery; but the moth is used to symbolise death, ants appear as symbolic of an individual's insignificance, etc.). Sound effects are used to emphasise the movement of the flea as it lands on a scalp in close-up and inserts its proboscis. We are reminded of the body horror of David Cronenberg and other fantasy horror films. Miette and One now confront the Siamese twins known as the Octopus on the deserted pier. The colour and quality of light here perfectly demonstrate the qualities of Darius Khondji's cinematography in the deep blacks of the sea and the acid yellow mist. There is a green tint that pervades the film that can also be seen in the nostalgic Montmartre of *Amélie*. There is also a feel of Hollywood melodrama in the composition and lighting design, a surreal distortion of the fantasy Hollywood *mise-en-scène* of the classic MGM musical. These overblown artificial sets and composition of the close-up shots could almost be from *The Wizard of Oz* (1939).

The character of the Octopus is a good example of the theme of bodily disfiguration and that runs through the work of Buñuel, Lynch and Švankmajer as well as that of Jeunet and Caro. The figure of the circus freak was also a feature of early Surrealist art, and the circus theme is also evident in the use of the trained flea that is now brought back into the action. The Octopus begins to play a tune using a hurdy-gurdy; this causes the flea (seen in extreme close-up) to release its phial of mind-control serum into One's scalp. The scale of the set and the way in which the ship dwarfs One is emphasised by the high camera angle. The circus melody now takes over from Badalamenti's more atmospheric score to add urgency to the next part of the sequence in which One begins to strangle Miette.

A sequence of chance actions now unfolds in a pictorial example of chaos theory as Miette's tear starts a chain of events, beginning with what was, at the time, a cutting-edge visual effect of a computer-generated tear flying through the air to land on a cobweb. This causes a spider to move, a bird to sing, a dog to bark and a drunk to throw a bottle. The bottle causes a seagull to defecate on a windscreen, making a car crash into a fire hydrant, releasing a torrent of water. The water sends rats into a nightclub, resulting in topless dancers running into the street. This distracts an electrician who plunges the city into darkness with the miraculous result of One and Miette being saved by a ship that crashes into the very pier on which they are standing.

Sound is effectively utilised throughout this scene in the manic laughter and ominous sounds of the port (foghorns, water, splitting wood, clanking steel) and also in the use of music mentioned previously. The camera work in this sequence emphasises extremities of scale: wide shots, high angles, low angles, extreme close-ups and point of view shots are all used to stylise the sets, distort characters and to focus on details that would be virtually unnoticeable if depicted 'naturally'. The *mise-en-scène*, in its restricted palette and nostalgic fantasy locations, is typical of the film as a whole and reflects the auteur signature of the directing team.

Critical Views

'The film seems to say that if you look a fairy tale in the eye, you're actually looking at a jungle of mixed-up mythology, religion, dreams and mind control. Even innocence isn't as innocent it seems.' (Stack, 1995, *San Francisco Chronicle*)

'A child smiles delightedly in his toy-filled room as Santa emerges from the chimney-piece, but joy turns to terror as the bearded visitor is followed by more of these, mind-controlled by a man screaming in a laboratory where, unable to dream himself, he has stolen the nightmare of a kidnapped orphan. The opening of another of Jeunet and Caro's forays into the *fantastique* is the perfect introduction to what's essentially a hugely inventive blend of dream, fairytale and myth, and to a strange, sinister sea-girt world that functions according to its own crazy logic.' (Pym, 2005, p. 234)

Filmography

Work by Jeunet and Caro

La Cité des enfants perdus (The City of Lost Children) (1995)
Delicatessen (1991)
Pas de repos pour Billy Brakko (1984) (directed by Jeunet but based on Caro's comics)
Le Bunker de la dernière rafale (1981)
Le Manège (1980)
L'Évasion (1978)

Films directed by Jean-Pierre Jeunet

Un long dimanche de fiançaille (A Very Long Engagement) (2005)
Le Fabuleux destin d'Amélie Poulain (Amélie) (2001)
Alien Resurrection (1997)

Foutaises (Things I Like, Things I Don't Like) (1989)

Films directed by Marc Caro

Dante 01 (2008)

Exercice of Steel (1998) (video short)

Méliès 88: Le topologue (1988) (television)

La Concierge est dans l'escalier (The Concierge is in the Stairs) (1987)

Rude Raid (1985)

Surrealism and Contemporary Cinema

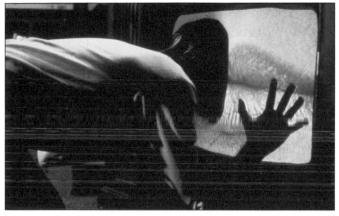

As discussed in the opening sections of this book, we can see the influence of Surrealism pervading contemporary popular culture at all levels. An interesting way to complete this study is to consider one contemporary director and one recent film that appear to be infected by the 'surreal virus' while managing to operate successfully within the constraints of the modern film industry, responding to the sophisticated demands of contemporary audiences.

David Cronenberg (Born 1943)

David Cronenberg is a Canadian film maker who is best known for the shocking nature of his 'body horror' films. Although his films often feature graphic scenes of violence or mutilation, they are not purely exploitative. Alongside expanding the nature of the horror genre, his work questions the nature of society and social relations.

He initially studied medicine at university whilst maintaining an interest in the arts and, after winning literary prizes for his written work, he transferred to an English course. After university, he travelled to Europe and on his return to Canada in 1966 started making short films. He helped set up the Toronto Film Co-op and became interested in underground and European cinema. After a couple of surreal shorts, his first major projects were experimental science fiction films. He soon moved into the mainstream, directing commercially successful horror films throughout the 1980s. He has continued to work outside of Hollywood as a Canadian film-maker, managing to blend mainstream genre work with his experimental tendencies.

David Cronenberg's career in many ways parallels that of David Lynch: they were born three years apart in North America, both distanced from the urban centres of the USA. They were brought up in fairly affluent middle class families and introduced to a broad range of art at a young age. Cronenberg's work could easily have developed in the same vein as Lynch and his initial influences were similar, approaching film as a medium for artistic expression. After a couple of surreal shorts, his first major project was made with the financial support of a writer's grant from the Canada Council for the Arts. *Stereo* (1969) was a black and white film exploring the topic of telepathy. After a few one-off screenings it gained a limited distribution and was followed by *Crimes of the Future* in 1970. These films began to develop a cult following and, like Lynch's *Eraserhead*, sat somewhere between the arthouse and late night horror market.

It is at this point in his career that Cronenberg decided that he wanted to reach a wider audience than avant-garde or experimental film promised. His subsequent work was to develop in the horror genre, using shocking techniques to explore issues and themes that the other surreal *auteurs*, discussed previously, have also entertained:

'(I) said to myself: "if you're going to do real movies, you're going to have to deal on some level with what the Cannes Festival represents. Maybe if I don't take it so seriously, it'll feel better." ... I knew I couldn't make movies like Stereo and Crimes and consider myself a professional film-maker. I also really wanted a broader audience. ... So I went back to Toronto and wrote the script for Shivers *(which I then called "Orgy of the Blood Parasites"). (Rodley, 1992, p. 54)*

Disillusioned with the idea of making personal, experimental films, he began more commercial work for Canadian television before eventually raising the finance to make his first successful horror film, *Shivers* in 1975. The film was popular with both reviewers and audiences but was heavily criticised in the Canadian media for its violent content (it features alien slugs who parasitically invade a luxury apartment block, causing the inhabitants to turn into nymphomaniac zombies). *Shivers* established his reputation as 'the king of body horror', able to create some of the most shocking and horrific images of the horror genre, infusing them with an element of social critique. 'Body horror' is the term used to describe horror films that have the mutation or mutilation of the human body at their centre (this was also one of Buñuel's themes).

Shivers was followed by *Rabid* (1977), which courted controversy not only in its content (an apocalyptic scenario of disease destroying a Canadian city), but also in the casting of a female porn star, Marilyn Chambers, in the lead role (perhaps a parallel to the early Surrealists' desire to shock). After the less successful drag racing film *Fast Company* (1979), he went on to write and direct another horror film with his then largest budget to date. *The Brood* (1979) is a horror story about a mother who creates a brood of small mutant murderers with gory results (a plot which Cronenberg admitted reflected his anger at his own divorce). His work was already dividing critical opinion; it was described by Roger Ebert as being 'disgusting in ways that are not entertaining' (http://rogerebert.suntimes.com) whereas Stephen Schiff described it as using horror as a 'new avenue of expression' (Walker, 2000, p. 116). These critical debates bring us back to the ideas raised previously about the 'value' of popular culture – can seemingly 'trashy' media products be considered in the same way as traditional art or literature dealing with the same themes?

His next film, *Scanners* (1981), costing an unprecedented 4 million Canadian dollars, was made quickly and under pressure but was an international success and brought him to an even wider audience. He followed this with one of his most fantastic and perceptive projects, *Videodrome* (1983). It caused outrage in the media, being described as 'dangerous when it is not risible' (Walker, 2000 p. 868). Its 'thoroughly tawdry concept' (Walker, ibid.) involves an interface between humans and machines, hardcore pornography and a pervasive criticism of modern society. Yet these themes have become ever more relevant with the advent of the internet. The film was not distributed widely despite being his first 'studio' film, and became his first commercial failure.

After reviving his commercial career via a successful big budget adaptation of Stephen King's *The Dead Zone* (1983) with producer Dino De Laurentiis (who would produce David Lynch's *Dune* in the following year), he was offered a free hand to remake the 1956 science fiction classic *The Fly*. Cronenberg's version (1986) was produced by Mel Brooks (who had also employed Lynch on *The Elephant Man* in 1980). *The Fly* combined strong casting (Jeff Goldblum and Geena Davis) with the 'body horror' of his earlier work and proved very successful at the box office, effectively moving horror into the mainstream via its overarching love story. He moved into more commercially uncomfortable territory with a subsequent project that had been six years in gestation and was difficult to attract commercial backers for. *Dead Ringers* (1988) is based on the true story of twin gynaecologists who both died of drug overdoses. The film deals with the themes of identity, disease, addiction and the body but lacks the explicit horror content of his earlier work. *Dead Ringers* was not particularly successful at the box office and again caused controversy due to its subject matter being read as pornographic and misogynist, the type of criticism that the early Surrealists would have courted.

Cronenberg's next project had an even longer gestation period and was potentially more controversial. As early as 1981 he had stated in an interview that he wanted to make a film of William Burroughs' cult novel, *Naked Lunch*. It is Cronenberg's most fantastically surreal work yet in its depiction of altered states of consciousness. The book itself had been subject to a censorship controversy in the 1950s due to its non-narrative portrayal of drug addiction and homosexual sex.

Like *Un chien andalou* before it, *Naked Lunch* (1991), is a collaborative venture involving two powerful creative personalities. Cronenberg wanted to develop a narrative from this difficult book by combining its imagery and content with biographical elements from Burroughs' life. He worked closely with Burroughs on the project and the film was a critical success. It had been said that the book could never be filmed and so it was quite a challenge to meet the expectations of the critics as well as reach a commercial audience. Burroughs' championing of the cut-up method for creating narrative is a direct descendant of the Surrealists' games discussed earlier. In 1996 Cronenberg yet again turned to more contentious subject matter with his adaptation of J.G. Ballard's novel,

Crash. Cronenberg's *Crash* is considered to be his most European-styled film, the closest he has yet come to the later style of cinematic Surrealism. Costello (2000) quotes J.G. Ballard as saying of the film '…the Surrealists discovered if you're going to present extraordinary subject matter, put your characters into dinner jackets' (Kubrick's *Eyes Wide Shut*, 1999, also takes this advice). The story involves a middle class couple who become involved in transgressive sexual acts and the perverse eroticism of car crashes, and was met with a firestorm of media controversy in the UK.

Following the controversial *Crash*, Cronenberg made some less successful outings before returning to a more subtly Surrealist social critique with *A History of Violence* (2005). This film is his most Lynchian in its depiction of violence and uncertain identity in small town America. The film parallels *Lost Highway* in the foregrounding of dual identity and the gangster as symbolic of an inescapably violent society. These themes pervade the apparent oxymoron that is 'American gothic': gothic representing the dark European history of medieval castles, cults and elaborate ornamentation; America being symbolic of the brave new modern world built on opportunity, technology and an expansive unsullied environment.

Gothic literature and film tends to have at its heart an element of fantasy, magic or the supernatural. The Surrealists tended to skirt around gothic themes, framing them within a melodramatic context and using elements of this hybrid genre to create an even more mutated offspring. The most successful gothic works tend to be those that show less visceral horror, preferring to build discomfort through omission, expectation and suspense. This notion is mirrored in *A History of Violence*, which takes the Surrealist tactic of creating emotional and psychological dislocation through the juxtaposition of disingenuous objects to a macro level. In the film we see small town rural family life juxtaposed with the violent world of inner-city gangsters, employing the device of one character with dual identities. These two stereotypes of American society are seldom co-joined to the extent that Lynch and Cronenberg use them; but when they are, the dream-like uncertainty of the narrative acts as a surreal disjunction that is effectively superior to overt fantasy.

As a Canadian, producing films for an international market dominated by American culture, Cronenberg's work can be seen as a dissection of this society – more specifically, the American psyche. The main character in *A History of Violence* (played by Viggo Mortensen) has two personas: the small town family man (Jack Stall) and the psychotic gangster (Joey Cusack). As the story unfolds, it becomes impossible for Jack to repress or hide his violent self indefinitely as his 'history' requires that he has to use extreme violence to protect his family. The final sequence of the film is the most powerful. He returns home after killing his mobster brother to a family evening meal in the kitchen of his rural home. Like an updated Ethan Edwards from John Ford's *The Searchers* (1956), it seems impossible that Jack could ever fit into a 'normal' domestic routine. There is little dialogue in the sequence but the tensions at the heart of American society and the violence that seems to permeate its history are laid bare more effectively than in any of Cronenberg's metaphorical body horror works.

Cronenberg's career has been a progression from the arthouse to exploitation movies, through big budget Hollywood to European stylised controversy and he appears to have pared down his style to negate the need for fantasy, horror or special effects. This reduction is at the heart of Surrealist cinema where the fantasy unsettles because it is inseparable from the cinematic reality. Although the (relatively) restrained content of *A History of Violence* is the antithesis of the fantasy content of *Naked Lunch*, its effect is more psychologically disturbing and, therefore, even more surreal.

Analysis of a short extract from *A History of Violence*

This sequence is taken from chapter 16 of the DVD release, at around 1 hour 24 minutes, and is the final scene of the film. Although Cronenberg's other films are far more shocking and fantastic in their content, it is worth looking at a sequence from this film to explore how he manages to create a subtly surreal atmosphere without resorting to the type of visceral horror for which he is famous (and which has spawned endless copycat video nasty exploitation films such as *Saw*, 2004).

The hero of the film, Tom Stall, has just killed his brother and is standing at the bottom of his brother's garden by a large lake. He throws his gun and bloodied shirt into the lake and kneels down to wash himself – a symbolic purification or baptism (religious themes have occurred earlier in the film when he talks about how he had previously disappeared in the wilderness and returned as a new man before meeting his wife and starting his new life). There is a wide shot,

 stretching to the horizon, the kneeling topless body of Tom suggesting a man in the environment – prone to the forces of nature. His blue denim jeans mark him out as the

American western hero attempting to purify himself and atone for his sins. There is a cut to a low angle close-up of Tom – his crucifix prominent in the shot, hanging from a silver chain around his neck. He looks worn-out and tired; he bears a guilt that he cannot wash away. The musical score (by Howard Shore – composer of the music for the *Lord of the Rings* trilogy) emphasises the emotion of the scene.

We cut to a white weatherboard farmhouse at night, icon of American rural family life, Tom's pick-up truck drives into shot; the pace of editing is slow. The *mise-en-scène* is realist, grey and dusty, as he emerges from his truck, he remains in the dark shadows – there has been no dialogue yet.

We cut to the interior of the farmhouse and are shown a series of shots of Tom's family. They are looking serious and concerned, pre-occupied with recent events as they sit in their family kitchen preparing to eat a meal. The wife, daughter and son have all been tainted by the violence that occurred previously in the narrative – we read their demeanour in the light of this knowledge. The interior *mise-en-scène* is that of a homely, middle-class rural American kitchen, there are pictures on the wall and family fridge magnets – all lit by low-key, subdued naturalistic lighting. The melancholy musical score continues.

We see Tom enter the home in long-shot, the family hesitate and look up before continuing the ritualistic preparations for their family meal. He walks slowly in, his head hung low, there is still no dialogue; the mood is expressed through the acting and the slow, subtle pace of editing. Tom stands in the kitchen doorway, we cut between Tom and his wife – they can't look each other in the eye. The tension continues to build as close-up shots are used to show the family looking around at each other; we are not sure what is going to happen next as

we continue to read this scene in the context of the violence that proceeded it. The blonde daughter (symbolising innocence and purity) stands up, takes a plate and lays a place at the table for her father. In long shot Tom approaches the place that has been laid for him and sits down. His wife appears to be praying or saying grace, her head is bowed. His son passes him a loaf, his head is hanging, his eyes are moist – he looks at his wife and their eyes meet: Is the emotion fear, relief or hope? It is impossible to tell – the film cuts to black and the credits roll. The characters cannot escape the violence, the history of which is referred to in the title – Tom's history and the wider society's history. This entire scene is executed with no dialogue – the communication is all through visual language and the grammar of the edit combined with an effective musical score.

This scene can be read in relation to one of the film's opening scenes; where Tom's daughter has a nightmare. He goes to her and says, 'There's no such thing as monsters – you were just having a bad dream.' Her brother supports this argument by explaining that, 'shadow monsters – look pretty scary but they really can't do anything.' We could read this as Cronenberg suggesting that the fantastic and shocking cinematic monsters that he has previously created are not as frightening as the 'monster' that stalks this film: the monster of the *History of Violence* is societal, criminal and institutional violence that cannot be escaped. The ending of the film is terrifying because it is uncertain: it is not particularly surreal or fantastic but it is all the more unsettling for the fact that it offers no answers.

Filmography

Eastern Promises (2007)
A History of Violence (2005)
Spider (2002)
Camera (2000/III)
eXistenZ (1999)
Crash (1996)
M. Butterfly (1993)
Naked Lunch (1991)
Dead Ringers (1988)
The Fly (1986)
The Dead Zone (1983)
Videodrome (1983)
Scanners (1981)
The Brood (1979)
Fast Company (1979)
Rabid (1977)
Shivers (1975)
Crimes of the Future (1970)
Stereo (1969)
From the Drain (1967)
Transfer (1966)

Charlie Kaufman & Spike Jonze and *Being John Malkovich* (1999)

Charlie Kaufman (Born 1958) and Spike Jonze (Born 1969)

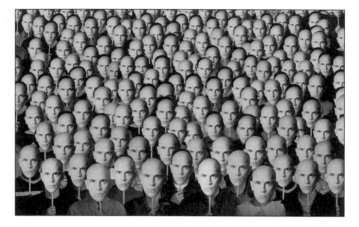

Cast

John Cusack: Craig Schwartz
Cameron Diaz: Lotte Schwartz
Catherine Keener: Maxine Lund
John Malkovich: John Horatio Malkovich
Orson Bean: Dr Lester

Mary Kay Place: Floris

Production Credits

Country: US/UK
Language: English
Producer: Michael Stipe and
                                 Sandy Stern
Director: Spike Jonze

Writer:	Charlie Kaufman
Cinematography:	Lance Acord
Editing:	Eric Zumbrunnen
Music:	Carter Burwell

Charlie Kaufman is a successful Hollywood screenwriter, renowned for his inventive and popular deconstruction of narrative conventions. His work often reflects upon the nature of social reality and of the narrative constructs used by Hollywood to create an illusion of reality. He started work as a journalist, moving on to write comedy sketches for television programmes. His first script was taken on by Hollywood producer, Steve Golin, who has a history of producing unconventional material (including David Lynch's *Wild at Heart*, 1990). Since the success of *Being John Malkovich* (1999), a number of his other highly inventive screenplays have been successfully produced, including *Adaptation* (2002) and *Eternal Sunshine of the Spotless Mind* (2004).

Spike Jonze originally worked as a music journalist before moving into the direction of critically acclaimed music videos for artists such as Weezer, The Beastie Boys, Fatboy Slim, R.E.M. and Björk. The interface between surrealism and advertising can be considered by examining these music videos alongside his successful advertising campaigns for Miller Lite and Adidas. He worked again with Kaufman on *Adaptation*.

Synopsis

An absurd black comedy in which an unhappily married puppeteer finds a filing job in a strange office block. At work he finds a portal that leads directly to the brain of the eponymous actor and which allows him to 'be' John

Malkovich. He teams up with another employee and exploits the portal for financial gain, leading him and his wife to question the nature of identity and consciousness as their relationship breaks down.

If any recent Hollywood film could be described as 'surreal' it would be *Being John Malkovich*. The film's premise is strange enough, focusing as it does around the idea that a secret passageway accessing the mind of John Malkovich exists between the seventh and eighth floor of a peculiar office block. The office scenario and *mise-en-scène* brings to mind *Alice in Wonderland* as Craig (the protagonist) appears to be the only one questioning the environment as it becomes 'curiouser and curiouser'. Craig is an artist and puppeteer (as was Jan Švankmajer); his obsession begins to extend into his ability to control the actions of other humans through the 'magical' portal, eventually using this power to develop his own fame and influence. The fantasy element of the film is never explained, leaving the audience uncertain as to its nature – forever vacillating on Todorov's border between what is real and what is supernatural.

One way to approach *Being John Malkovich* is to look at the work of the scriptwriter, Charlie Kaufman. In many ways, the film supports screenwriter William Goldman's argument that the author of a film can be any one, or a combination of, the key production crew and that 'movies are a group endeavour' (Goldman, 1983, p. 102). In the case of *Being John Malkovich*, the scriptwriter appears the most likely candidate for *auteur* status.

Kaufman is responsible for a number of film scripts in which memory and identity are key themes: *Eternal Sunshine of the Spotless Mind*, *Confessions of a Dangerous Mind* (2002) and *Adaptation* (2002). The debutant director of *Being John*

Malkovich, Spike Jonze, doesn't have a particularly strong visual style or technique – much of the surreal and fantasy content comes from the film's premise and its script. As Craig says in the film, the idea of a portal into someone's brain opens up a 'metaphysical can of worms' – it raises all sorts of philosophical questions about identity and the nature of self. These themes are played out as an absurd comedy with the obvious jokes about self-important actors disappearing up their own portals. (Comedy was one of Buñuel's preferred modes. He is known to have disliked irony and favoured broader comedy as a way to question social mores.) The film was a critical and modest commercial success, reflected in its three Oscar nominations. It is also an insider's film about the movie-making process as much as it is an exploration of identity.

Being John Malkovich is therefore an interesting film through which to examine how far the language of independent or avant-garde film making has infiltrated mainstream Hollywood movies. There are many films that deal with disjointed narratives, particularly since the success of *Pulp Fiction* (1994), but most films will conform to generic conventions. *Being John Malkovich* stands outside of mainstream genres; it could only really be described in conventional generic terms as a comedy – but it's not a *conventional* comedy. The fact that Michael Stipe (lead singer of rock group R.E.M.) produced the film, coupled with Jonze's background in music videos, might lead detractors to point towards a fairly superficial 'pop' background to the movie. It is easy to see the language of Surrealism turned to the service of capitalism by watching television advertising breaks.

Another criticism aimed at Kaufman is that he makes self-referential films that are 'totally reflexive, about screenwriting itself' (James, 2004, p. 17). He has worked with director Michel

Gondry who, like Jonze, has a background in directing stylish music videos. Rather than considering how the film sits outside generic conventions, we should consider whether it fits the conventional Hollywood storytelling mode or the 'three act structure'.

Being John Malkovich and the three act structure

As generic divisions have dissolved in contemporary Hollywood, the idea of the 'high concept movie' has evolved – this is a film that can be summed up in a simple sentence and that follows a conventional structure organised around three 'acts':

Act One – The setup or 'hook'

This will take the first 15 to 30 minutes of a film in which we are introduced to the main characters, their function in the narrative and their goals. The main obstacle to the protagonist's development will be introduced (usually in the form of an antagonist). The idea of Act One is to engage the audience's attention and set up questions that will hopefully be answered as the narrative develops.

Act Two – The development

In the middle section of the film (usually the longest act) the protagonist begins a cause/effect journey, encountering obstacles and false hopes until, at the end, all seems lost. As an audience, we are asking 'how is he/she going to get out of this?'

Act Three – The conclusion

The final section of the film involves a climax where the different narrative strands come together in the form of a confrontation between the protagonist and antagonist. This confrontation will result in a resolution to the narrative – it is in this resolution that the film's ideology can be identified. The conventional Hollywood narrative will have a happy ending.

If we now consider *Being John Malkovich* in the above way, we should start off with the tagline of the film: 'Ever want to be someone else? Now you can'.

This concept is developed through the film's narrative as follows:

Act One

We meet Craig the struggling artist/puppeteer (protagonist) and his wife Lotte. Craig has to get a boring office job where he meets Maxine (the antagonist) and discovers the Malkovich portal.

Act Two

A series of questions and obstacles are created that involve a sequence of cause/effect relationships: Craig and Lotte fall for Maxine who uses both to her own ends; Malkovich himself finds out about the secret passageway; they all take it in turns to use the portal to control Malkovich and each other. Putting aside the fantasy element, the major focus of this act is the developing relationship between the main characters. Act Two ends as Lotte discovers that Dr Lester intends to use

Malkovich to attain immortality for himself and his friends. The final act begins to get even more hectic as the plot spirals out of control.

Act Three

Craig takes complete control of Malkovich and uses his celebrity to develop his career as a puppeteer. Maxine becomes pregnant and through a spoof documentary, we see that Malkovich has given up acting to become a puppetry guru. Malkovich comes home from a performance to find that Dr Lester has kidnapped Maxine. Craig refuses to help liberate Maxine resulting in a chase through Malkovich's subconscious memories. Maxine tells Lotte that she is the 'father' of her baby. Craig decides to leave the portal from which he is controlling Malkovich in order to save Maxine but the two women leave him at the roadside while Dr Lester and his friends all enter Malkovich's portal. Seven years later, an older Malkovich shows his friend that the new portal will be Maxine's daughter, Emily. We see that Craig has become trapped in Emily, the film ending with Emily swimming under water.

Although the content of the film may seem obscure (and it is difficult to describe) it still actually fits the pattern of the high-concept three act structure. It is a wonderfully absurd film that illustrates how inventive storytelling can create a plausible universe from an implausible concept and is a good film to use in order to consider the nature, influences and extent of Surrealism in mainstream cinema. In many ways it illustrates how classical Hollywood narrative devices can be used to tell any story, no matter how bizarre. This can be seen in opposition to the way that Buñuel's *The Phantom of Liberty* wages war on storytelling itself by undermining conventional narrative devices.

Analysis of a short extract from *Being John Malkovich*

This sequence is taken from Chapter 21 of the DVD release, in which John Malkovich discovers and visits the portal into his own brain. The scene opens as Malkovich follows a small group of clients to floor $7\frac{1}{2}$ of the office block where Maxine and Craig work. The set for floor $7\frac{1}{2}$ has been created with a low ceiling; a drab, grey interior with strip lighting – similar to any number of urban office blocks. It is reminiscent of Švankmajer's Soviet-inspired shorts such as *Dimensions of Dialogue* where bureaucrats sit at desks in anonymous soviet offices. The claustrophobia and de-humanised atmosphere are emphasised by the queue of people waiting quietly to enter the portal, bent double due to the low ceiling – they are also reminiscent of the subterranean workers in Fritz Lang's *Metropolis*. Švankmajer's *Alice* appears to be referenced in the next shot as we see a small, worn Victorian-style door at floor level, too small for a human to walk through. Malkovich pushes past the queue and bursts into the room where Max and Craig are collecting money, controlling the entrance to the portal. Malkovich appears angry and egotistical; we can see Kaufman (the scriptwriter) developing a theme here – the power of the artist/actor in contemporary Hollywood and the effect that this has on their sense of celebrity/importance.

We cut to a low-angle view from inside the portal. The

cramped, claustrophobic atmosphere is reiterated as the characters bend to look into the doorway. Malkovich peers into the doorway, we then see his point of view as he crawls towards the camera down the dark, earthy organic tunnel. As Craig watches him disappear, he delivers a line of dialogue that seems to sum up one of the main themes of the film and could be its alternative tagline:

> 'What happens when a man goes through his own portal?'

Maxine's response reveals the peculiar dynamics of the relationship between Craig and Maxine. Craig is uptight, serious and concerned about the implications – he appears somewhat cowardly and uncertain. Maxine, however is self-assured and relaxed, she appears to control the relationship as she replies:

> 'We'll see!'

The question of 'who is pulling the strings' in terms of relationships and narrative dynamics is another theme that runs through the film.

Malkovich continues to crawl through the dark tunnel towards the light at its end when we hear a rushing sound and the door slams shut behind him. Special effects similar to those found in the horror genre are then employed to accelerate the viewer toward a point of view shot of a neatly laid table in a restaurant. With its silver service, napkin and glass of wine, it is a framed symbol of bourgeois life. The formal meal is used as a plot device in the films of Cocteau (*La Belle et la bete*), Jeunet and Caro (*Delicatessen*), Švankmajer (*Little Otik*) and Cronenberg (*A History of Violence*), but it is in Buñuel's films where the theme of the middle-class meal as a social convention is fully developed. This happens specifically in *The Discreet Charm of the Bourgeoisie* where the desire to eat this symbolic meal is never consummated.

The camera continues with Malkovich's point of view as it tilts up from the table to a voluptuous female body in a low-cut dress; the tilt continues upwards to reveal that she has the head of John Malkovich. She takes the form of an 'exquisite corpse' (the Surrealist game of chance in which an image is built up in collaboration – one person drawing the legs, the next the body and a third the head). In this case the tilt reveals that the figure is constructed from a neatly laid table, a voluptuous female body and a bald man's head. She begins to speak, saying only the word 'Malkovich' repeated endlessly, it is the only word uttered in this scene, the utterances taking the form of a meaningless Dada poem. This scene uses computer-generated effects to create a strange, confusing dream image as Malkovich sees that everyone in the restaurant has his head and they are all muttering 'Malkovich'. The scene doesn't appear to be diegetically 'real' – it only makes sense as a dream or psychological hallucination. It seems to be a Surrealist *hypnagogic* scenario as he runs around the restaurant bumping into himself; filmed using frenetic handheld camerawork. This 'dream sequence' has the feel of a music video – it is similar to Chris Cunningham's 'Windowlicker' video for Aphex Twin (2002) where the women all have the face of Aphex Twin (Cunningham is a contemporary of Jonze – both of the them highly successful as experimental music video makers).Malkovich pushes open the restaurant doors that open into a bright light; he then falls into the night time roadside of the New Jersey turnpike. The camera techniques in this sequence combine elements of the high concept thriller with more experimental video effects and *mise-en-scène* to develop a disturbing vision of an obscure concept. The power of Malkovich's persona and theatrical technique acts as a foil to Cusack's weaker character and the fantastic nature of the narrative.

Kaufman's scripts tend to contain stories within stories that fold in on themselves. In this film we could see the portal as a metaphor for the creative process through which the film-maker attempts to control the actor in order to realise his (or her) vision. In this case, the film is nominally about being John Malkovich, yet Malkovich has no real role as a driving force in the narrative – he is used as a puppet to explore themes of significance to the scriptwriter (possibly the nature of fame, the role of the actor, relationships between creative individuals and 'the system', the nature of consciousness and the role of narrative, etc.). In this sequence from the film, we see a fantasy vision of what could happen if the actor took control of this creative process in which he is 'merely' an actor. As Malkovich says at the end of the sequence:

> 'That portal is mine and it must be
> sealed up forever — for the love
> of God!'

Critical Views

'What an endlessly inventive movie this is! Charlie Kaufman, the writer of "*Being John Malkovich*," supplies a stream of dazzling inventions, twists and wicked paradoxes. And the director, Spike Jonze, doesn't pounce on each one like fresh prey, but unveils it slyly, as if there's more where that came from. Rare is the movie where the last half hour surprises you just as much as the first, and in ways you're not expecting. The movie has ideas enough for half a dozen films, but Jonze and his cast handle them so surely that we never feel hard-pressed; we're enchanted by one development after the next.' (Ebert, 1999, *Chicago Sun-Times*)

'"*Being John Malkovich*" is the first produced screenplay by Charlie Kaufman, and it bears the mark of demented

genius. This is a movie that adamantly refuses to observe the conventions of cinematic storytelling or succumb to real-world logic. It's a gleeful, nitrous-oxide high, midway between a Monty Python sketch and a Buñuel film, with dream-like structure and pseudoscientific charts to match.' (O'Hehir, 1999, *Salon Magazine*)

Appendix – Answering Examination Questions on Surrealist and Fantasy Cinema

Questions set on this topic may take a number of approaches to what is a broad and undefined subject area. Below is one example of an examination question with a worked answer. Other questions may focus on one of the following areas, but in all cases you should reflect on your own experience of studying these films:

1. When watching Surrealist cinema, how important is it to have knowledge of the films' context (e.g. national, *auteur*, genre)?

2. What are the key differences between Surrealist and fantasy film?

3. How unusual or extraordinary is the *content* of the films you have studied – how do we make sense of the film (audience study)?

4. How unusual or disorientating are the storytelling techniques used (narrative structure)?

The answer to the question below has the following structure:

1. **Introduction:** An introduction that defines the terms 'conventional narrative cinema' and 'Surrealist and fantasy film'.

2. **Context:** A brief outline of the history of Surrealism.

3. **Development:** Luis Buñuel as a surreal *auteur* – making the link between the roots of Surrealism and surreal cinema.

4. **Illustration:** Using *The Phantom of Liberty* to illustrate the points made previously.

5. **Further development:** Surrealism in contemporary Hollywood using *Lost Highway* as an example.

6. **Alternative illustration:** *Little Otik* as an example of a fantasy film with supernatural content but a more conventional structure.

7. **Conclusion:** Reviewing points made earlier and showing an understanding of the way that film language develops over time and how non-linear structures and complex characterisation have become more acceptable in contemporary narrative cinema.

Question

"In what ways do Surrealist and fantasy films challenge our usual expectations of conventional narrative cinema?"

In responding to this question is it first worth considering a definition of conventional narrative cinema: films are normally expected to be approximately 90 to 120 minutes in length; they will usually feature a limited range of clearly-defined character types who we can identify with and who follow a narrative journey. This narrative will have a clear resolution and the main characters will have developed in some way through this experience. A conventional narrative film may be shot in a broad range of cinematic styles using (for example) invisible continuity editing and realist locations or montage editing and fantasy locations. The key difference between conventional narrative films and Surrealist cinema is not an

attack on our expectations of film style but on our expectations of stories, characters and social conventions.

The Surrealist movement was one of a number of radical art movements that developed in the first half of the twentieth century. Unlike other movements such as Futurism, Cubism, Constructivism or Dada, the name of Surrealism has entered common usage and is most likely in fact without used as an adjective to describe all sorts of films, television programmes, photographs and novels. We are also likely to use the word to describe events in our life that appear to combine fact and fantasy. Surrealism initially developed as a literary movement; it combined Dada's nihilism with Freudian psychology in an attempt to change the world for the better by unleashing the 'power of the unconscious'. The Surrealists attempted to do this through games and techniques of chance such as automatic writing, word association, 'consequences', doodles and collage. The influence of Surrealism soon grew to encompass the visual arts and it became inevitable that the relatively new medium of cinema would become attractive to the Surrealists. The early Parisian Surrealists would wander from one cinema to another absorbing extracts from different stories and combining them in their heads to form a new narrative from these juxtaposed elements.

Luis Buñuel is the most prolific and long-lived of Surrealist film-makers in that he was present at the birth of Surrealism in Paris in the 1920s and was still making films over 50 years later. His first film, created with Salvador Dali, was *Un chien andalou*. This film was written by the two film-makers in tandem, sharing their dreams and then combining these to form a surreal narrative. The film uses shocking effects such as a razor slicing an eye (created by clever use of editing and a prosthetic eye); it also has wilfully obscure inter-titles that seem to follow melodramatic conventions and yet make little

conventional narrative sense. To this obscure mix is added the political radicalism of the Dada and Surrealist movements; religious and sexual taboos are broken as we see the clergy dragged along the floor attached to dead donkeys as well as fetishised images of breasts, buttocks and pubic hair. We can consider *Un chien andalou* as an early experimental film – playing with the language of film as much as the content. We can also see parallels between some of the effects used in this film and the big budget blockbusters of contemporary Hollywood: for example, the scene in *Un chien andalou* where a man's mouth disappears can be seen recurring in *The Matrix* where Neo's mouth is removed (temporarily) by Agent Smith. The cutaway (to a cloud passing over the moon), used to convince us that the sliced prosthetic eye is 'real', can be seen as a standard example of continuity editing used in contemporary horror films where gruesome special effects are the norm.

Although *Un chien andalou* may have been challenging when it was first screened, it now seems more of a historical artefact than a real challenge to our expectations of conventional narrative cinema. It may be a better comparison to look at one of Buñuel's last films from the 1970s such as *The Phantom of Liberty*. This film is shot in a sparse style with very little use of Expressionist lighting, close-ups or montage editing. The film concentrates on attacking our expectations of narrative flow; it is constructed from a series of vignettes or sketches, each connected to the next by a minor character who goes on to become the major character in the next sequence. It deals with a range of unusual topics such as incest, child abduction, cancer, murder and sadism in a style that relates more to the melodrama of soap opera rather than the prurient horror that the topics might suggest or that you might see in the films of, for example, David Cronenberg. The film's real challenge is not the subject matter, much of which is autobiographical, but the structure and characterisation. In *The Phantom of Liberty* there are more than 40 characters, none of whom follows a traditional character arc – most of the stories are just starting to get interesting when they are left with no resolution. In one scene, a character is given a letter by a postman who appears in his dream. Just as we are about to discover what is in the letter, the story moves on to another character and does not return. At the end of the film we are left with more questions than answers. The film does not follow any of the standard conventions of narrative or character and challenges us to confront our expectations of what a feature film is and what type of stories we expect from cinema.

We can also see some of these themes developed in the work of contemporary Hollywood film-makers. David Lynch has created a body of work and a personal style that appears to connect directly with the themes of Surrealism. His films deal with subjects that we might find in many contemporary Hollywood films such as crime, sexual deviancy, violence and fantasy. What sets Lynch's films apart is his use of fractured identities and dream-like narratives; these ideas match the Surrealist tactics of challenging conventional characterisation. Lynch also tends to use the language of mainstream film genres but creates his own 'Lynchian' universe. A good example of this is his film *Lost Highway*: this film uses slick Hollywood production values and the Star System (it features Bill Pullman and Patricia Arquette). Lynch describes the movie as a 'noir horror film'; it is quite a dark film and contains a number of gruesome sequences such as man's head being impaled on a glass coffee table. None of these elements in themselves sets the film out as a challenge to our usual expectations of narrative cinema; what gives the film its surreal nature is the multi-layered narrative and the confusion of identities. We are never sure why or how Fred Madison turns into Pete Dayton, we are not told how the two Patricia Arquette characters relate to each other – we see a photograph of the two characters together, but at the end of the film one of the incarnations has disappeared from the same photograph. We are left with a film that appears to be a mystery without a resolution or a fantasy without an explanation. In a conventional mystery film, there may be bizarre characters and unexplained events, but at the end of the film, these events have (at least to some extent) been explained. Even in conventional fantasy films, the fantastic or supernatural makes sense in the film world or to the characters in the narrative. But in *Lost Highway*, we are offered no simple explanations.

Some Surrealist and fantasy films take a more conventional approach to narrative, one such example being Jan Švankmajer's *Little Otik*. This film takes a traditional folk tale and updates it to take place in the contemporary Czech Republic. The story follows a childless couple who turn an unearthed tree root into a substitute baby. The root comes to life and continues to grow, devouring first animals and then people. Although the film combines live action with animation and is quite heavily stylised with regular use of extreme close-ups to emphasise themes, it doesn't challenge our expectations in terms of narrative or character. It follows a linear path with a limited number of key characters involved in a series of strange events that lead to a clearly-defined conclusion. In fact it follows the conventional Hollywood narrative arc with its conflict/resolution pattern.

Film language is constantly developing, the techniques that once shocked or confused audiences can soon become tired clichés with little impact. Many contemporary Hollywood films will use non-linear narrative techniques to tell complex stories about multiple characters, two examples being films such as *Crash* (2004) or *Magnolia* (1999). There has been a tendency in what is commonly called arthouse cinema to disrupt conventional narrative, to make time flow backwards or loop the same events through multiple viewpoints (for example, *Last Days*, 2005; *Elephant*, 2003; *Memento*, 2000; *Irreversible*, 2002; *Code: Unknown*, 2000; *Primer*, 2004, etc.). This would suggest that surreal and fantasy techniques have in many ways become part of the mainstream and are no longer able to challenge our expectations. The real challenge that Surrealist and fantasy films present us with is in the way that they make us question our expectations of stories and characters, making us feel uncomfortable and making us question social conventions or the idea of simple definitions of identity or morality. We normally expect to feel comforted by a cinematic experience with its conventional 'happy ending'. The real challenge of Surrealist cinema is its refusal to offer any kind of ending – what Roland Barthes called 'the terror of uncertain signs'.

Bibliography

Aranda, F. *Luis Buñuel: A Critical Biography* Secker and Warburg (1975)

Barthes, R. *Image-Music-Text* Fontana (1977)

Baxter, J. *Buñuel* Fourth Estate (1995)

Buñuel, L. *My Last Breath* Flamingo (1983)

Buñuel, L. *An Unspeakable Betrayal* University of California Press (2000)

Carrière, J-C. *The Secret Language of Film* Pantheon (1994)

Chion, M. *David Lynch* BFI (1995)

Costello, J. *David Cronenberg* Pocket Essentials (2000)

Donald, J. (ed.) *Fantasy Cinema* BFI (1989)

Fowler, C. (ed.) *The European Cinema Reader* Routledge (2002)

Gelder, K. (ed.) *The Horror Reader* Routledge (2000)

Goldman, W. *Adventures in the Screentrade* Futura (1983)

Gooding, M. (ed.) *A Book of Surrealist Games* Shambala (1995)

Hayward, S. *Key Concepts in Cinema Studies* Routledge (1996)

Hopkins, D. *Dada and Surrealism: A Very Short Introduction* Oxford University Press (2004)

Kinder, M. (ed.) *Luis Buñuel's The Discreet Charm of the Bourgeosie* Cambridge University Press (1999)

Lacan, J. *Ecrits: A Selection* Routledge, 2001

Instituto Cervantes *Buñuel 100 Years: It's Dangerous to Look Inside* MOMA New York (2000)

James, N. 'I Forgot to Remember to Forget' *Sight and Sound* Vol. 14(5), pp. 14–18 (May 2004)

Katz, E. *The Macmillan International Film Encyclopedia* (3rd Edition) Macmillan (1998)

Marx, K. and Engels, F. *The Communist Manifesto* Penguin Classics (1985)

Montagu, J. *The Surrealists: Revolutions in Art and Writing 1919-35* Tate Publishing (2002)

Mulvey, L. 'Visual Pleasure and Narrative Cinema' *Screen* 16 (3), (1975), pp. 6–18

Paini, D. (ed.) *Cocteau Jean Centre* Georges Pompidou (2003)

Pym, J. (ed.) *'Time Out' Film Guide* Time Out (2005)

Rodley, C. *Cronenberg on Cronenberg* Faber and Faber (1992)

Rodley, C. 'David Lynch, Mr Contradiction' *Sight and Sound* 6(7), pp. 6–10 (July 1996)

Rodley, C. *Lynch on Lynch* (revised edition) Faber & Faber (2005)

Sinclair, I. *Crash* BFI (1999)

Sitney, P. *Visionary Film: The American Avant-garde 1943-1978* Oxford University Press (1974)

Tasker, T. *Fifty Contemporary Film-makers* Routledge (2002)

Turner, G. *Film as Social Practice* Routledge (1999)

Tzara, T. *Seven Dada Manifestos and Lampisteries* John Calder (1981)

Vincendeau, G. 'Miss France' *Sight and Sound* 15(2), pp. 12–15 (February 2005)

Waldberg, P. *Surrealism* McGraw-Hill (1971)

Walker, J. (ed.) *Halliwell's Film and Video Guide 2001* Harper Collins (2000)

Wells, P. *Understanding Animation* Routledge (1998)

Wood, M. 'Down With Liberty' *Sight and Sound* 10(9), pp. 30–3 (September 2000)

Internet Sources

Alda, C. (2006) *'Long Strange Trip'* Prague Post. Available from: http://www.praguepost.com/articles/2006/12/06/long-strange-trip.php [Accessed 20/02/07]

Berardinelli, J. (1995) *'City of Lost Children'* Movie Reviews Collosus. Available from: http://movie-reviews.colossus.net/movies/c/city_lost.html [Accessed 06/02/05]

de Bruyn, D. (2002) *'Chasing Rabbits out of the Hat and into the Shedding of Childhood'* Senses of Cinema. Available from: http://www.sensesofcinema.com/contents/cteq/02/20/alice.html [Accessed 21/03/05]

Corman, R. (1965) *'Surrealism and my Films'* Other Cinema. Available from: http://www.othercinema.com/otherzine/otherzine4/pcorman.html [Accessed 11/03/2005]

Ebert, R. (1995 & 1999) *'City of Lost Children'* & *'Being John Malkovich'* Chicago Sun-Times. Available from: http://rogerebert.suntimes.com [Accessed 14/03/05]

French, P. (2004) *'Why this Orpheus will always Live On'* The Observer. Available from: http://film.guardian.co.uk/News_Story/Critic_Review [Accessed 17/03/05]

Gonzalez, E. (2003) *'The Phantom of Liberty'* Slant Magazine. Available from: http://www.slantmagazine.com/film/film_review.asp?ID=809 [Accessed 09/03/05]

Lanzagorta, M. (2002) *'The Phantom of Liberty'* Senses of Cinema. Available from: http://www.sensesofcinema.com/contents/cteq/02/20/phantom.html [Accessed 11/03/05]

O'Hchir, A. (1999) *'Being John Malkovich'* Salon Magazine. Available from: http://www.salon.com/ent/movies [Accessed 21/03/05]

Russell, J. (2004) *'Orphée'* BBC Films. Available from: http://www.bbc.co.uk/films/2004/02/25/orphee_1950_review.shtml [Accessed 17/03/05]

Schlockoff, A. Karani, C. (1995) 'Excerpts from a Conversation with Jean-Pierre Jeunet and Marc Caro' Sony Pictures. Available from: http://www.sonypictures.com/classics/city/misc/interview.html [Accessed 16/03/05]

Stack, P. (1995) 'Odd but riveting "children"' San Fransisco Chronicles. Available from: http://www.sfgate.com/cgi-bin/article.cgi?f=/c/a/1995/12/22/DD68295.DTL [Accessed 20/04/07]

Švankmajer, J. (1999) *'An Alchemist's Nightmares'* Kinoeye. Available from: http://www.kinoeye.org/02/01/svankmajer01.php [Accessed 20/02/07]

Švankmajer, J. (2001) *'Out of my Head'* Guardian Newspaper (19 October 2001). Available from: http://film.guardian.co.uk/features/featurepages/0,4120,576459,00.html [Accessed 20/02/07]

Zacharek, S. *'Highway to Heck'* Salon Magazine. Available from: http://archive.salon.com/feb97/highway970228.html [Accessed 21/03/05]

Selected websites of directors and films featured

http://www.luisBuñuel.org/inicio/Buñuel1.html Official Buñuel site (in Spanish).

http://www.filmref.com/directors/dirpages/Buñuel.html Brief information on a number of Buñuel's films (in English).

http://www.davidlynch.com/ David Lynch's official site – with original web-only content (for members).

http://www.netcomuk.co.uk/~lenin/Jean_Cocteau_Index.html A useful Cocteau-related site.

http://www.davidcronenberg.de/ A German Cronenberg site, mainly in English with some good information and essays.

http://jpjeunetlesite.online.fr/ Official site of Jean-Pierre Jeunet (in English and French).

http://www.lynchnet.com/lh/ Official page for Lynch's *Lost Highway*, with press kit, film clips and interviews.

http://www.sonyclassics.com/city/ Official site for the Sony release of *City of Lost Children*.

http://www.criterioncollection.com/asp/release.asp?id=68&eid=17&section=essay Interesting essay on Cocteau's *Orpheus* from the American distributor's site.